LEGAL RESEARCH METHODS

Michael D. Murray
Valparaiso University School of Law

and

Christy Hallam DeSanctis
The George Washington University Law School

FOUNDATION PRESS

2009

THOMSON REUTERS

© 2009 By THOMSON REUTERS/FOUNDATION PRESS
195 Broadway, 9th Floor
New York, NY 10007
Phone Toll Free 1–877–888–1330
Fax (212) 367–6799
foundation–press.com

Printed in the United States of America

ISBN 978–1–59941–396–9

TEXT IS PRINTED ON 10% POST CONSUMER RECYCLED PAPER

ABOUT THE AUTHORS

Michael D. Murray is Associate Professor of Law at Valparaiso University School of Law. He has taught at the University of Illinois College of Law from 2002 to 2008, and Saint Louis University School of Law from 1998-2002. He teaches law school and undergraduate courses in Art Law, Civil Procedure, First Amendment and Censorship, International Art and Cultural Heritage, International Civil Liberties: Freedom of Expression, Introduction to Advocacy, Legal Research and Writing, Legal Writing and Analysis, and Professional Responsibility. Professor Murray is the author or coauthor of fourteen books and several law review articles on art law, civil procedure, copyright, freedom of expression, law and the health care professions, legal research and writing, and products liability. His casebook, ***Art Law: Cases and Materials*** (2004), is one of the most widely adopted casebooks in the field. Professor Murray graduated from Loyola College in Maryland and from Columbia Law School, where he was a Harlan Fiske Stone Scholar. He was a member of a national champion Jessup International Law Moot Court team at Columbia, and Notes Editor of the Columbia Journal of Transnational Law. After law school, he clerked for United States District Judge John F. Nangle of the Eastern District of Missouri and Chair of the Judicial Panel on Multidistrict Litigation. Murray also practiced commercial, intellectual property, and products liability litigation for seven years at Bryan Cave law firm in St. Louis.

Christy H. DeSanctis is Associate Professor of Legal Research and Writing and Director of the Legal Research and Writing Program at the George Washington University Law School. The Program encompasses 1L Legal Research and Writing, and Introduction to Advocacy; the Scholarly Writing and LL.M. Thesis Programs; and an in-house Writing Center. After graduating from NYU School of Law, she clerked for John W. Bissell, the former Chief Judge of the U.S. District Court for the District of New Jersey. Prior to joining the GW faculty, Professor DeSanctis practiced at the Washington, D.C., law firms of Collier Shannon Scott and Steptoe & Johnson. There, she focused on trial and appellate litigation at both the state and federal level, including in the U.S. Supreme Court, and worked on a variety of regulatory and legislative matters before federal agencies and Congress. She also published numerous articles relating to major legislative efforts with which she was directly involved, including terrorism insurance legislation and federal health and financial privacy regulations. Professor DeSanctis began teaching as an adjunct faculty member at GW in 2002; she was appointed to the fulltime faculty and assumed the Directorship of the LRW Program in 2004. In addition to teaching legal research and writing courses, she also teaches Law and Literature. She regularly speaks at conferences on legal writing and rhetoric. Professor DeSanctis also has taught several undergraduate English courses at the University of Maryland, College Park, including: Introduction to the Novel; American Literature after 1865; and Freshman Composition, a persuasive writing course based in part on theories of classical rhetoric. In addition to her J.D., Professor DeSanctis holds a Masters in English language and literature with a minor in rhetoric and composition from the University of Maryland. She is currently at work on a Ph.D. in late nineteenth and early twentieth century American Literature.

DEDICATION

To Denise, Olivia, and Dennis, who make it fun;

To my sisters, Margaret, Mary, Jeannette, Anne, and Laura, who proved to me that the benefits of a teaching career outweigh all the costs.

M.D.M.
St. Louis, MO
March 2009

To Michael B. DeSanctis, as always;

To my friends and family who have put up with me for all of these years.

C.H.D.
Washington, DC
March 2009

ACKNOWLEDGMENTS

This book is a continuation of the LRW Series at Foundation Press that we, the authors, started four years ago. We have had a great deal of assistance from editors and others at Foundation Press over the past eight years. In particular, we would like to thank Robb Westawker, who steered this current interactive book project through the production process at Foundation Press, and Heidi Boe and Bob Temple for their part in making it come to fruition. We continue to thank John Bloomquist, the Publisher of Foundation Press, for five years of helping us through each of the stages of publication, marketing, and sales of our books. And we remember fondly Steve Errick, formerly Editor of Foundation Press, for being the first to latch on to our book proposal and for never giving up on it.

Several other people also are owed our gratitude for their unwavering support of our professional endeavors and participation in the process resulting in this book. Professor Murray would like to single out his research and teaching assistants: Sasha Madlem, Robin Martinez, Tyler Pratt, and Vanessa Sheehan at Valparaiso University School of Law; Lindsay Beyer, Brian George, Aaron Goldberg, and Maurice Holman at the University of Illinois College of Law, and Renee Auderer, Jeannie Bell, Jonathan Blitz, John Challis, and Katalin Raby at Saint Louis University School of Law. We also thank the students who allowed us to use their work as writing examples: Lindsay Beyer, Jessica Bregant, Michelle Chen, Jim Davis, Jeffrey Ekeberg, Ken Halcom, James Klempir, Suleen Lee, Gerald Meyer, Greg Rubio, Vaishali Shah, Ellen Shiels, Gabriel Siegle, Joshua Watson, and Jim Williams at the University of Illinois College of Law; and Jeannie Bell, Kevin Etzkorn, Josh Knight, Kirsten Moder, Allison Price, Gaylin Rich, Jerrod Sharp, Katherine Weathers, and Cherie Wyatt at Saint Louis University School of Law. Special thanks also are due to Professor Murray's assistants over the last eight years, Kristin Takish at Valparaiso University, and Mary Parsons and Deanna Shumard at the University of Illinois, whose support above and beyond the call of duty is remarkable and much appreciated.

Professor DeSanctis would like to recognize Jessica L. Clark and Kristen E. Murray, for their outstanding assistance running the GW LRW Program in past years, friendship, unabashed humor, and superb insight on how to teach students to write well; Professor Lorri Unumb, my predecessor at GW, for teaching me not only how to teach legal writing but also how to run a great program; and all of the GW Law Dean's Fellows and Writing Fellows from 2004 to 2008 for their energy and unceasing desire to make teaching legal research and citation interesting, rewarding and fun (and the 2004-05 Writing Fellows in particular for their assistance with the Appendix in this text on grammar rules).

The authors thank their legal research and writing colleagues who reviewed and commented on the text: Kenneth Chestek (University of Indiana-Indianapolis School of Law); Jessica Clark (George Washington University); Jane Ginsburg (Columbia Law School); Terri LeClercq (University of Texas School of Law); Pamela Lysaght (University of Detroit Mercy School of Law); Joanna Mossop (Columbia Law School); Kristen Murray (Temple University, Beasley School of Law); Suzanne Rowe (University of Oregon School of Law); Ann Davis Shields (Washington University School of Law); Judith Smith (Columbia Law School); Mark Wojcik (John Marshall Law School); and Cliff Zimmerman (Northwestern University School of Law). This book is the better for their kind and generous review and input.

Professor DeSanctis also thanks the following people: Linda A. Shashoua for her unwavering support in this endeavor and all of my others, as well as her guidance, friendship, and expertise in putting thoughts into both writing (and music!); Michael S. Levine, for his seemily undying friendship (despite my attempts to ignore him) and for sharing with me his thoughts and insights from almost ten years of teaching legal writing; George D. Gopen, for teaching me everything I know about reader and listener expectations; the Hon. John W. Bissell, for the opportunity to work with a true wordsmith; Scott A. Sinder, for teaching me how to write anything in one hour (and a Supreme Court brief in a weekend! (extenuating circumstances)); Pam Chamberlain for her institutional know-how and priceless advice on how the GW program operates; and to all of the past, present and future GW LRW adjunct professors (including, in no particular order: Lisa Goldblatt, Tom Simeone, Ken Kryvoruka, Andrew Steinberg, Josh Braunstein, John Arnett, Andrea Agathoklis, Tim McIlmail, Donna McCaffrey, Scott Castle, Bill Goodrich, Susan Lynch, Erik Barnett, and many others, from whom I have learned and continue to learn an enormous amount about a practice-oriented approach to teaching legal writing). And, oh yes, Michael DeSanctis – you simply cannot be a better writer than he is, hands down (*how* do you so masterfully edit things that you know nothing about?).

PREFACE

This book is a part of Murray and DeSanctis's Legal Research and Writing Series of books at Foundation Press, the latest titles of which are interactive texts providing a print format of the book and an electronic format that is enhanced with pop-up definitions, callout boxes, linked documents and presentations, and internal and external hyperlinks to expand the capacities of the text beyond the four corners of each page.

The three, new, interactive titles in the series are: *Legal Writing and Analysis*, *Legal Research Methods*, and *Advanced Legal Writing and Oral Advocacy: Trials, Appeals, and Moot Court*. These books teach legal method, which consists of the skills necessary to determine legal issues (legal questions that need to be answered) from a given situation or set of facts, to research the law that speaks to these issues, to analyze the law, and to communicate the legal analysis or to advocate a client's position based on the legal analysis. The 1L legal method, legal research and writing, or introduction to advocacy course usually is the first course to teach law students these skills directly and to evaluate a student's progress in learning them.

The Interactive Casebook Series is designed for the current generation of law students whose familiarity and comfort with on-line and computer-based learning creates a demand for teaching resources that take advantage of that familiarity and comfort level. The first two interactive legal research and writing texts will provide a process-based legal methods course book and a legal research text covering all aspects of first year legal analysis, research, and objective legal writing topics. The third text is designed for second semester and upper-division advanced writing courses involving advocacy and oral argument at the trial and appellate levels and in moot court competitions.

Paired with the course books will be electronic, computer-based versions of the texts that add links to on-line databases and internet-based resources and supplement the text with pop-up definitions, graphical and textual explanations and depictions, and presentations to introduce and summarize the material. The electronic versions of the text will be fully searchable and highly portable, and each page can be annotated or highlighted. The table of contents and each of the chapters will contain internal and external navigation links, making them more valuable for use in class and out.

The Interactive texts will employ a layout that departs from the traditional, all-text casebook format through use of callout text boxes, diagrams, and color/border segregated feature sections for hypotheticals, references to scholarly debates, or other useful information for law students. Call-out topics include: Food for Thought; FYI; Major Themes; Make the Connection!; Point-Counterpoint; Do it with Style!; Apply it!; Take Note!; What's that?; and Practice Pointer.

These texts will deliver a process-oriented approach to writing and analysis in objective and adversarial contexts supplemented with product-based analytical tools. The texts will cover objective office memoranda and client letters as well as pretrial motions (motions to dismiss and summary judgment motions), writ petitions, and appellate briefs, and oral argument at the trial and appellate level. The texts are designed by professors with substantial practice experience, employing advanced rhetorical techniques, Explanatory Synthesis, and multiple annotated samples of work product.

CONTENTS

Chapter 1

Introduction to Legal Research

Lawyers do not go to law school to learn all the law they will need to practice law. That is an impossibility. It is a complete non-starter. It simply cannot be done. The law changes daily and there are some topics within the law that are covered by volumes of statutes, regulations, and other legal sources that practically no one ever could memorize. At most, law school teaches future lawyers how to think about problems in a way that allows them to discern the legal implications of different facts and situations—often called "learning to think like a lawyer." Law school also teaches basic principles of bedrock areas of the law—torts and contracts and criminal law and the like—the kind of basic principles that run through many discreet areas of law and, partially for that reason, are tested on every state's bar exam. This ensures that lawyers have a certain minimal level of competence with regard to the most common areas of the law and legal problems. But the third thing law school teaches lawyers is how to find the correct sources of the law and teach themselves the current law that governs the problem before them. This is known as the process of legal research.

This book will addresses the process of legal research and will examine in detail the sources of the law available on-line, through web-based research services, and in print form. This first chapter introduces the process of legal research to answer specific legal questions and the major categories of source materials used in legal research.

FYI

Don't be fooled by anyone who tells you that researching "in the books" is a forgotten science. First of all, it's not, especially when you are researching the intricacies of a specialized area of law. But, second, and perhaps most importantly, we care more that you understand research as a process. Book research naturally lends itself to a process-oriented approach; mere "Google-searching" (looking only for hits on your highlighted terms) does not. That is *not* to say that we disfavor electronic resources or electronic searching. We do not. But there is a certain scientific approach to legal research that risks being lost in the "Google generation." That is, it is generally *not sufficient* simply to find key highlighted terms in primary and secondary sources. Rather, you must take a step back and embark on a methodological approach to answer the legal questions you have been asked to address – whether you are doing on line research or print research – and really think about what you want to know and where you might go to find the answers. If you limit yourself to looking for mere word and phrase matches in the terms that you initially conceive of, you are destined to overlook important resources that can answer your legal question more thoroughly (and correctly).

THE PROCESS OF LEGAL RESEARCH

I.   INITIAL ASSESSMENT OF THE PROBLEM

A.   Fact Gathering

Every research project starts with a problem. Your client, who at

---

FOOD FOR THOUGHT

At some point in the not too distant future, a supervisor in your law office may walk into to your office or cubicle and give you a discreet legal issue to research.

"Jane, I want you to research the statute of limitations on a claim of strict products liability for failure to warn in the state of Alabama."

"Bob, go and look up the elements of a claim of defamation in New Hampshire."

When you wake up from this pleasant dream, you will realize that this situation is exceedingly rare. What really happens is that a client or a colleague or supervisor tells you about a problem.

"This guy has put a trailer on my land and he looks like he is going to stay there and live in it indefinitely. What can I do about it?"

"Our client, Mary Quitecontrary, was filmed by a surveillance camera at her cubicle at her place of work while she was eating a plate of ribs, and she got a little messy eating, and someone there, she doesn't know who, took a clip of the footage and dubbed it and made it into a kind of fake commercial. Well that person, we don't know who, put the thing on YouTube. What can we do for her?"

At this point, your job is to gather the facts, determine what questions have to be answered (the legal issues) in order to render advice on the matter, and then go and gather the correct sources of the law that will answer the issues, and analyze these sources so as to reach your conclusions and communicate them to the client.

---

this moment may be your boss or a more senior colleague in the office, tells you a story—a set of facts that describe a certain situation—and the client thinks legal research will be necessary to answer one or more questions suggested by the fact situation. Your first job is to gather enough facts so that you can begin to assess the problem.

We are not going to spend a great deal of time talking about fact gathering. Some of the fact-gathering processes already may be familiar to you (calling or meeting with knowledgeable people to interview them, looking for facts on the internet or in other repositories of facts, and gathering information from public sources such as libraries and government agencies), and other parts of the process will be explored in other law school courses (taking discovery if the matter is in litigation, client interviewing and counseling, and the more esoteric and specialized means of fact gathering, such as Freedom of Information Act requests). The goal of fact gathering is to be able to identify the issues—the specific legal questions that need to be answered—then to determine if additional facts are needed from the client or other sources, and finally to put together a plan of action to find the legal sources necessary to answer the questions.

B.   Determining what is at issue

When considering a set of facts presenting a legal problem, your first question should be, "Do I know what is at issue in this problem?" If you can answer this question at the outset because the facts immediately suggest to you specific legal questions in specific areas of the law, then you can move on to the tasks of gathering additional facts (if needed) and planning out your research to answer the questions. You are in the comfortable position of knowing one or more areas of the law well enough to take a new fact pattern and identify what areas and topics within the areas are implicated by the facts and to formulate specific questions to answer based on the facts.

However, the specific questions to answer may not occur to you while you are reading or listening to the facts.

APPLY IT!

Step into the process we are describing with the problems we presented earlier in this chapter:

"This guy has put a trailer on my land and he looks like he is going to stay there and live in it indefinitely. What can I do about it?"

Does this suggest to you an area or more than one area of the law that might govern this situation? Do you even have specific legal questions in mind that should be answered in order to render legal advice to this client? Perhaps you are thinking of words to describe this situation, such as "squatter" or "trespasser." All of these may be useful in proceeding with your research on this problem. Now consider the second scenario:

"Our client, Mary Quitecontrary, was filmed by a surveillance camera at her cubicle at her place of work while she was eating a plate of ribs, and she got a little messy eating, and someone there, she doesn't know who, took a clip of the footage and dubbed it and made it into a kind of fake commercial. Well that person, we don't know who, put the thing on YouTube. What can we do for her?"

The same questions may be posed: do you know the area of law? Do you have any specific legal questions to answer based on these facts? Are you thinking of any key words, such as "privacy" or "embarrassment" or "exploitation" or "emotional distress" that might lead you in certain directions in your research? This thought process is the first step in preparing to research an answer to these problems.

You may have an idea about which areas of the law are implicated by the problem (e.g., this sounds like a fraud case, or this probably is a copyright case), but you will not necessarily know enough about these areas of the law and their fundamental background principles, claims, defenses, and policies to be able to determine the specific legal questions you need to answer. You may not even know the general areas of the law implicated by the problem. Assuming the "client" cannot shed any light on this (or has left the assignment in your in-box and cannot be reached), you will need to do background research into the law.

C.   Background research into the area of law

If you do not know what areas of law are implicated by the problem, let alone specific legal questions to answer, you will have to start your research broadly. You have facts, so start with the facts. Look up some of the words from the operative facts in a legal dictionary or legal ency-

PRACTICE POINTER

Determining Search Terms
There is a basic procedure to starting any research project regardless of whether you are starting your research on-line or in the books: you must generate search terms. Search terms are key words and phrases that you will input into the search boxes of on-line and electronic resources and databases, or that you will look up in the index or table of contents of a print source. Where do you get them from? Generally, you get them from the facts and circumstances of the problem. Some terms may be associated with the persons or entities involved (a land owner, a tax payer, a thief), some may be associated with the places or things involved (a parcel of land, a sum of money, a stolen painting), some may be associated with the actions of the persons or entities (an offer to sell, a failure to pay, the removal of the painting without permission), while others will be derived from the law itself and the terms associated with the claims and defenses of the applicable rules of law (negligence, breach, assumption of risk, absence of malice). To determine search terms that are derived from the area of law, you must know the area fairly well, which points to the need to do background research into the area of law to gain such understanding. Your goal is to determine good search terms—those that will point you to the correct sources of the law in the most efficient and cost-effective manner.

In our problems above, you may decide that "squatter" and "property" and "occupy land without permission" are good search terms for the first problem, and "workplace," "employee," "invasion of privacy," and "surveillance camera" are potentially useful search terms for the second problem.

These terms are just the starting point. Research, as the name indicates, is a process of searching and re-searching based on what you learn from prior searches and how you can use that knowledge to refine your search terms as you progress along and learn more and more about the law governing the problem at hand.

clopedia. As with most modern sources of the law, legal dictionaries and encyclopedias have on-line and print versions.

Legal dictionaries, such as <u>Black's Law Dictionary</u>, define legal terms of art and many other words that appear in legal settings. The definition of a simple word from your facts, such as "privacy" or "employee" or "surveillance" may point the way to several areas of law that should be investigated in order to zero in on the actual issues you will need to answer.

Legal encyclopedias, such as <u>Corpus Juris Secundum</u> and <u>American Jurisprudence</u> attempt to present the entire law of a certain jurisdic-

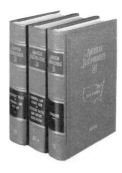

tion (<u>Corpus Juris Secundum</u> and <u>American Juris-prudence</u> target the whole United States) in a topic by topic outline format. An encyclopedia's scope is extremely broad, but the depth of its coverage of any given topic necessarily is limited. At most, you will learn the black letter law concerning the various claims, defenses, issues, and policies that are at work in the area. The indices to the encyclopedia will point you to various legal areas for background investigation into the law. You can start in the index with a few key words like those above—privacy, employee, surveillance—and the index will tell you what areas of the law might be implicated by these facts.

When you have a background resource, you will read it to answer the following questions:

- What are the major issues in this area of the law, both old and new?

- What are the kinds of claims, injuries, damages, causes of action, and defenses that are brought or claimed or asserted in this area?

- What constitutional issues are implicated (if any)?

- Are there statutes, rules, or administrative regulations that typically are found in this area?

The information you find in a dictionary or encyclopedia may help you get your feet wet, but you may exhaust what they have to say on your matter without determining the actual issues that are implicated by your facts. You will have to go deeper, to hornbooks, treatises, and practice guides.

Treatises are books or binders written by one or more legal scholars and are devoted to a scholarly presentation and discussion of the law in a specific area, such as torts, contracts, insurance law, class actions, or securities regulation. In print form, they often are written in several volumes, if not dozens of volumes, as in the case of Wright and Miller's <u>Federal Practice and Procedure</u>. The level of discussion tends to be intense, and it is targeted to legal scholars and lawyers, but law students generally can figure out what's going on through careful reading and re-reading.

Hornbooks are a one volume treatise on a certain area of the law, such as Calamari and Perillo's Hornbook on Contracts, and are specifically designed for use by law students and lawyers alike. Hornbooks will try to cover the same type of information as a treatise, but they necessarily are constrained by their one-volume page limit in the depth to which they can discuss each topic and subtopic of the law.

Practice guides, with titles such as New York Products Liability 2d or <u>California Practice Guide: Family Law</u> are specifically written for practicing attorneys, and out of respect for the time pressures of this audience, they attempt to present the most important information needed by practitioners in the area in a succinct manner, without going into great detail of discussion or explanation of all the nuances of the legal area and its major topics and subtopics. Because they take such a direct approach, practice guides can be perfectly adequate to supply your need for general background information on the issues, causes of action, defenses, constitutional and statutory treatment, and policies of the area of the law, but in other instances you will need a more thorough source, and you will look for a treatise.

<u>Annotated law reports</u> have an important function in finding relevant cases on specific legal topics, and they can be written in a similar style as an encyclopedia, although each annotation is narrowly focused, and there is not necessarily an annotation covering every topic you would like to investigate. Annotations are designed to collect and report cases and other primary authorities on the specific topics they discuss, rather than to analyze or critique the law of the area. In that annotations specifically are designed for use as a case finder, they are less use-ful than a treatise or practice guide in teaching you a broad foundation of legal principles and black letter law in a given legal area, although they

can be very useful if you are looking for citations to relevant cases from multiple jurisdictions.

<u>Law review articles</u> probably are not a good place to get grounded in an area of law. The typical well-written article is a narrowly focused work with incredibly detailed analysis. Compared to an encyclopedia, a typical law review article is an inch wide and a mile thick. Instead of delving into such deep waters at the start of your analysis of a problem, you should start out with more reasonable resources, such as encyclopedias or practice guides, and move on to a treatise.

Law school casebooks are not particularly useful for gaining a foundation in a specific area of the law in a reasonable period of time. There is nothing wrong with consulting a casebook on the topic, but these texts primarily are designed to teach law in a certain methodical way, case by case, showing examples of the development of the law and highlights of the big issues, so that a law student can learn to think about the law in general and this area of the law in particular. Cases are chosen because of what they say and how they demonstrate the historical and intellectual development of the law, not necessarily because they represent the prevailing authority in any jurisdiction. This organization is not conducive to quickly identifying your questions about the topic.

Avoid commercial study aids—Nutshells, Gilbert's, Emmanuel's and the like—when you are taking on a legal problem in preparation for research. These study aids are meant to help you learn an entire course of study in the law, and although they are quicker to consult than a casebook, they will not point you to  all of the issues implicated by an actual legal problem that exists in an actual jurisdiction and is governed by that jurisdiction's law. Encyclopedias, practice guides, and treatises do not take that much longer to consult, and they will provide you with more complete information to set you off on your research task.

All of the background authorities discussed above will cite statutes and cases, and it is a good idea to start reading the statutes and case law from your jurisdiction as you come across these authorities to see examples of how the overall rules work in specific situations. Aside from that, in the background research stage, there is no need to run a search on-line for statutes or cases or to pick up a statutory compilation or case digest and actually use their descriptive word indices to identify topics relating to your facts and then to use these topics to find statutory sections or cases in your area. This will soon be your task when you get down to actual research, but at this point, you are just trying to identify the issues.

At the end of your self-guided introduction to an area of law, you will need to return to your facts and determine the specific questions that are presented by these facts. If you still cannot do this, return to the background material. You might also discover a need for additional factual information from your client or other sources.

D.   Additional background research into the facts

After becoming grounded in a new area of the law, you may determine that your boss or the client did not give you enough factual information to address the issues intelligently. Go back and ask them for more information. Assuming that they have disclosed all the information that currently is available to them, you may have to perform your research with what you already know or, with certain kinds of factual information, you can turn to alternative sources of information.

As a college graduate with a bachelor's or higher degree in one or more academic disciplines, you no doubt are aware of many sources of factual information, whether it be informational, archival, technological, statistical, historical, or geographical. Search engines on-line tap into virtual databases and brick-and-mortar libraries on the ground contain resources that are obvious places to turn to if you need technological information about the field that your client is involved in so that you can understand the facts of the legal sources you will be studying. You may need geographic information about the place involved in the facts—What is there? What does it look like? You may need historical information about your client's situation—What led up to this situation? Has this problem been going on before my client got involved? Has this problem come up before and been resolved in a certain way? Other more specialized information is kept in various depositories. You might need, for example, archived information of the local Recorder of Deeds' office regarding a piece of real estate, or statistics from the local Department of Health.

E.   Background information of the "how to do it" kind

When you leave the friendly confines of law school and move on to practice, you may soon find yourself in need of "how to do it" information in a new area of the law. For example, your client is a creditor of a personal estate, but you don't know how to intervene in the probate case or file an adversarial claim against the estate. Your client may be in a domestic relations case where a guardian needs to be appointed, but you have no idea how to go about getting a guardian appointed. Or your client has a claim against a bankrupt debtor, but you have no idea how to prepare and file a proof of claim. "How to" sources include:

1.   Your colleagues, and other lawyers you know

Your colleagues and other attorneys can be the shortest and most direct path to this practical information. Ask people who have done it before, and hopefully they can teach you to avoid the mistakes and pitfalls of the area. Unfortunately, as a law student, you most likely do not have knowledgeable colleagues that you can consult even if the professor would let you do this on a law school assignment, so you will need to try other avenues.

2.   Practice guides and practice-oriented continuing legal education (CLE) materials

Practice guides and <u>CLE materials</u> are drafted for practitioners. They are written to assist practitioners who already practice in the area of law covered by the guide and those who are new to the area. Because they are so practice-oriented, these guides will provide you with "how to do it" information about drafting a demand, or raising defenses, or preparing a claim in that area of the law. Sample pleadings, discovery, contracts, wills, and other documents often will be provided as models from which to work. Law students should be careful to follow whatever model is provided by their professors rather than one found in a guide book, but if none is presented, the guides can show you rudimentary forms for many legal documents.

3.   The agency or court

If you are making your first foray into the Division of Family Services, the Probate Court, or the Equal Employment Opportunity Commission, do not be intimidated about calling up the agency or court and asking, "How do I do something?" You may have to call several times to get the right person to answer your questions, but the right person often can tell you what you need to know and provide you with the right forms to use.

4.   Pleading and practice form books

Speaking of forms, if that really is all you need, there are books devoted to this topic. Form books are particularly useful for somewhat obscure practice areas like admiralty law—if you are told, for example, that you have to go "arrest" a ship, you will need certain forms of pleadings and documents to accomplish this. The first time you have a case in one of these areas you will be feeling your way along in darkness, and form books at least can shed some light on the paperwork involved in the process.

II.   PLANNING YOUR RESEARCH

After formulating the questions you must answer, you must develop a plan for finding the sources to answer each issue. You should divide your plan into categories—how are you going to find:

- Primary controlling authorities

- Primary persuasive authorities

- Secondary authorities

- Sources for checking and validating your authorities.

It is advisable to write up a plan of action for your research and follow it. Write down the sources you will use and the order in which you will use them. Leave space in your plan outline to make notes on what you checked and what you found.

Writing a plan makes you focus on the task at hand. It forces you to get organized. It reveals gaps in your plan when you finish jotting it down and have a look at what you came up with. And it will keep you honest—your written plan will remind you to do the job properly, as you planned it, so that you can check off all the items and complete the plan.

Keep a good record of every item (every individual authority) that you find, including what it says and the citation of the authority and page number where you found the material. This will save you hours of frustration in the future when you cannot find the same book on the shelf, or the library is closed, or you cannot quite remember the name of the case you read on-line that said something crucial about a certain element of a legal rule.

A well-prepared record of the findings also can be used as a skeletal outline of your written work product, which you later can flesh out and turn into a proper treatment of the issues. For example, as you research, you probably will learn that there are a certain number of required elements for the rule on the issue, and two or three exceptions to the rule, and a number of defenses to the rule. Writing down this information about the rule in your notes will create a skeleton outline of the rule section of your written work product. As you find authorities that provide the sub-rules, factors, policies, considerations, or simply provide explanation or clarification of any of the items in the outline, you can fill in the information as a rough outline of the explanation sections of the treatments of the main issue and the elements of the rule. Then, when you stop, you will have a fairly complete skeletal outline of the actual work product you will draft. If you can fill in the skeletal outline on a computer as you go along, your conversion of the skeletal outline to a fully detailed outline or even the actual paper will be even easier.[1]

III.   PERFORMING THE RESEARCH

A.   Determining the scope of the research

In the real world outside of law school, the research plan you devise will depend in part on the time allotted or money allocated to the project by you, your boss, the client, or the court. You cannot always adopt a "leave no stone unturned" plan in which you will try to completely exhaust every possible source for the law. Sometimes the deadline set by your boss or the court is too short for that; other times, the client simply cannot or will not afford that level of research. You may find that this is particularly true where on-line fee-based research (Westlaw or Lexis) is involved. So time and money are important factors in actual law practice.

Another factor is your knowledge of the area of the law. If you know the area well, you will not have to look for authorities in as many places and you can zero in on the sources you know are likely to lead you directly to the answer. When you are familiar with the area, you will feel more confident when you think you have found the right answer so that you can stop your research. The converse is true when you are less famil-iar with the area of law—you will need to look to more sources to find authorities and you may not be as confident when are trying to decide whether you should stop your research.

---

1 This method saves time in the long run, but there is an up front investment of time (and the client's money) that might not be justified if the project is sufficiently simple or the deadline is drastically short or the client cannot or does not want to pay you for this level of work. A good example is if the client (or your boss) just wants an oral answer to the question and tells you not to spend more than four or five hours on it. Don't worry about a carefully prepared research plan that you will methodically fill in to create a skeleton outline of your work product. Just go and find the authorities.

B.   Forming search terms for research

The process of research in on-line and print sources of the law is the same: you must derive search terms from your issues. These key words and phrases will be used as search terms for on-line resources or will be looked up in the indices or tables of contents of print sources.

1.   Catch words, concepts from legal issues

When you are given a legal problem and you set off to find sources that discuss this legal problem, the first thing to do is to break your problem down into catch words, legal concepts, or brief phrases that summarize the legal issues (legal questions) implicated by your problem. The gateway to most printed legal sources is their indices, and the indices are organized into alphabetical lists of key words, brief phrases, and legal concepts. The gateway to on-line sources is their search function that allows you to access the sources in their databases, or a search engine that searches for sources on the World Wide Web.

When you are determining search terms, consider terms relating to:

- the parties—the people and entities involved in the problem;

- the actions, transactions, or events, and things or items involved in the problem;

- potential liability between the parties and defenses to liability;

- potential relief obtainable in actions between the parties.

For example, if the problem you are given is the following: **A hunter with a rifle runs into someone's home in pursuit of a running deer and trips and falls and discharges his weapon injuring a housewife,** then the first thing to do is to break the problem down into concepts, catch words, and brief phrases:

Hunter, hunting, and negligence [party, action, potential claim for liability];

Weapons, guns, rifles and negligence with guns; weapons in household or indoors; accidental discharge of weapon; accidental shooting [actions and items involved in the problem];

Trespassing and negligence while trespassing; liability for damage or injury to property owner [potential liabilities to a party]

What did we leave out?—**deer; pursuit/hot pursuit of quarry; running with guns; tripping; housewife.** Perhaps the first couple of terms (deer, hot pursuit, running with guns) might turn up a case or two, but probably not a statutory provision. Use your discretion. The latter words and concepts (tripping, housewife) are probably dead ends. Experience will help you make the determination of what to look up and what to leave out.

2.   Search for these words, concepts, and phrases

The leading on-line resources devoted to legal research, Westlaw and Lexis, have search functions to search their databases. The difference between their search functions and the average internet search engine is that you are able to craft more precise searches employing what is known as Boolean logic (expressing logical connections between search terms, such as "within five words" of another search term or "within the same sentence" as another search term). For example:

dog /3 bite   Will pull up any document where the word "dog" shows up three words ahead of or behind the word "bite."

dog +2 bite   Will get you documents where "dog" precedes the word "bite" by no more than two words.

dog /s bite   Will pull up any document in which "dog" appears in the same sentence as "bite."

Chapter 3 and Chapter 8 discuss other attributes of Westlaw and

Lexis's search functions that allow your searches to be more logical and precise than those created for the average internet search engine.

The indices to printed legal sources, often called descriptive word indices, list and cross-reference search terms and other related key words, concepts, and short phrases. Even if you do not come up with the exact key word from your problem, you often will find a cross-reference that leads you to the correct term. E.g., "gun" will cross-reference you to "weapons;" "dog" will cross-reference you to "animals;" "hunting" will cross-reference you to "negligence–sports and recreation."

3.   If you come up short, search more broadly and think of synonyms

If you cannot find cases using the most promising words and concepts, broaden your inquiry into these other areas. Read all the sources your turn up using the word "Hunting." Read further in the sources uncovered by the terms "Weapons" or "Guns." Think of synonyms for your initial words and concepts and search for them.

Synonyms expand the possible words an authority could contain and thus allow broader results from your search:

hunting, stalking, chasing, sport

weapon, gun, rifle, pistol, bullet

home, house, household, indoors

shoot, shot, shooting, accident, discharge, "went off," fire, killed

negligence, negligent, liable, culpable

C.   Legal research sources

We briefly mentioned several of the sources you will use in your actual legal research. By way of further introduction, we will describe these and other sources in this section.

SOURCES FOR PRIMARY AUTHORITIES: STATUTES AND CONSTITUTIONS

Statutory Compilations, Annotated and Unannotated

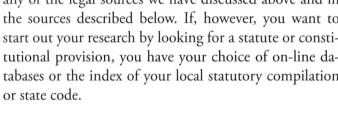

You can find references to statutes or constitutional provisions in any of the legal sources we have discussed above and in the sources described below. If, however, you want to start out your research by looking for a statute or constitutional provision, you have your choice of on-line databases or the index of your local statutory compilation or state code.

Federal and state constitutions generally are accessible for free in federal or state government sponsored websites, e.g., the United States Constitution, http://www.gpoaccess.gov/constitution/ or the Rhode Island Constitution, http://www.rilin.state.ri.us/RiConstitution/. The same is true for federal and state statutes, e.g., the United States Code,   http://www.gpoaccess.gov/uscode/ or the New Mexico Statutes, http://nxt.ella.net/NXT/gateway.dll?f=templates$fn=default.htm$vid=nm:all, although most often you are given free access only to the "official" or unannotated version of the statutes.[2] The annotations and other research tools for the statutes are part of the value added by a private legal publisher, and the publisher will want to be paid for this effort (see Chapter 2 for more information). If you are lucky, the website will allow you to search for key words within the text of the constitution or statutes; otherwise you will have to scan an on-line table of contents or index.

In print, constitutions generally are found in statutory compilations or codes, e.g., the United States Constitution is printed with the United States Code; the South Carolina Constitution is printed with the Code of Laws of South Carolina, and key terms—legal words and concepts—are listed in the indices to the statutes and codes that refer you to constitutional and statutory headings and citations that pertain to the specific topics that have been covered by the constitution and statutes in your jurisdiction. You also can peruse the list of headings in the table of contents to the constitution to see if the subject matter of your issue is

---

2 But see the Wyoming Statutes, http://legisweb.state.wy.us/titles/statutes.htm, providing free access to the unannotated and annotated versions of the statutes.

covered by one or more constitutional or statutory sections.

The same process applies whether you are working with annotated or unannotated versions of the statutes on-line or in book form. Annotated versions simply add excerpts and citations to cases and other authorities that have applied and interpreted the statutory section you are researching. The annotations are roughly organized like a mini-digest on the topic of the particular statutory section at hand, and like digests, they are very important case finding tools (see Chapter 3 infra).

SOURCES FOR PRIMARY AUTHORITIES: CASES

On-line Databases and Print Reporters

Reporters, such as the Federal Reporter, New York Miscellaneous Reports, and Missouri Cases, actually contain the opinions and orders of courts that you will study in order to determine the law. However, you will not be able find all of the relevant cases just by pulling reporters off the shelves. Each volume of the reporter series will contain mini-digests and tables of cases and other reference information, but it is much more beneficial to use other "case finder" resources to locate the citations to the cases you should research, and then to look them up in the reporters.

Westlaw and Lexis

The case law databases on Westlaw and Lexis are the bread and butter of these services. Their collections of case law in all American jurisdictions are exhaustive and comprehensive, so you can run a search with the confidence that if you use the correct search terms you will find the correct cases. If your firm and your clients can afford it, Westlaw and Lexis can provide one-stop shopping for potentially controlling case authorities.

TAKE NOTE!

Have you ever heard the expression, "Garbage in, garbage out"? In legal research, this phrase points to the critical need to use good search terms. If the search terms you are using do not fully encapsulate the critical terms of the area of law of your problem, there will gaps in your results.

General Internet Search Engines

Who doesn't love Google? We, the authors, certainly are tantalized by it, and in fact we really do not know anyone who does not love the quickness and convenience of Google in finding specific pieces of information or simply grabbing a random source for a fact you are trying to pin down. The trouble with this approach alone as a formula for legal research is that in legal research you are not trying to find one or two specific pieces of information and you are not looking for random sources for facts. The goals of legal research actually have little in common with the goals of a typical internet search. In fact, it is inapposite to describe legal work as "a search." You are not looking for one decent search that turns up some useful tidbits. Rather, you want to search, to re-search, and to re-search again and again until you have assured yourself that you have the correct answer.

Stated otherwise, when you search Google or one of the other general interest search engines, you can be, and often are, satisfied by finding one source that appears to speak to the item your were researching. Everything from the democratically created knowledge of Wikipedia to the contents of a Facebook page or a college student's blog can serve as a "source" when all you are looking for is a little reassurance that you have gotten your facts straight. In legal research, in contrast, you must be able to access (and assess) *all* of the relevant, potentially controlling authorities. There is nothing random about the authorities you must find. And it is not enough to find a few or even a bunch of controlling authorities; you must exhaust the controlling authorities on the issue so that you can be sure that you have not missed any developments or changes in the law.

Our efforts here attempt to dissuade you from falling back on the simple and the familiar in your legal research. If you simply want to find a single case or a single statutory or constitutional provision when you already know the name of the case or what the provision does or should say, then by all means use Google or another search engine. But when you are doing "full-blown" legal research in law school or on behalf of a client, stick to the resources we are describing in this chapter that are designed to allow you to do complete, exhaustive, appropriate research on any given legal issue.

Digests

Whether you access them in print or on-line, when using print resources, digests are the first and foremost "case finder" resource. Digests contain lists of excerpts from cases (West Group's digests are lists of headnotes from the cases West has published) organized by key words from these cases, and by various legal concepts, short phrases, and terms of art. As with all legal research, you start your research by breaking down your issues into key words and legal concepts, and then refer to the digest index to determine under which digest topics to look for cases. One of the nicest things about digests is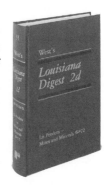
that they are organized by region (national, regional, or state), or jurisdiction (federal vs. an individual state), or subject matter (e.g., bankruptcy, military law) so that you can zero in on the best cases for your problem.

Annotated Law Reports

Annotated Law Reports (ALR) likewise are available in print or on- line. In either medium, they are a print "case finder" resource made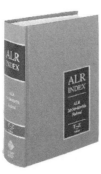
up of reports called "annotations" on certain specific legal topics, with dozens and dozens of citations to cases in that area. Often the publication of an annotation on a given topic is prompted by the issuance of an important case in the area, or by the emergence of a conflict between courts or jurisdictions regarding a certain area of the law. The reports really are just text written so as to have a place to hang all the footnotes citing to the cases; there rarely is any synthesis of these authorities attempted in the reports, and unlike a treatise or law review article, you generally will not find a thesis or even the author's point of view on the law. As a result, ALRs do not carry much weight as secondary persuasive authorities. This should not trouble you, however, because you most often will refer to an ALR annotation to get the current law in a specific area and to find the prevailing authorities that support the current law, not to cite the annotation as authority in and of itself. Because the law moves on and the cases become dated and sometimes are overturned or superseded by more recent authorities, annotations are updated or superseded from time to time.

Encyclopedias and Practice Guides

We have placed encyclopedias and practice guides together not because they are similar in nature but because we have adequately described them above. Encyclopedias and practice guides primarily are used as background material to obtain an initial footing in an unfamiliar area of the law. Either source can be used to find cases, but unless the encyclopedia is drafted for your particular jurisdiction, reference to cases from your jurisdiction will be accidental at best. A general encyclopedia is a good background resource, but it is not the right place to pin down the prevailing authorities in any one jurisdiction. Practitioners and judges alike sometimes cite the national encyclopedias, Corpus Juris Secundum and American Jurisprudence, for basic black letter principles of an area of the law, but reliance on these sources as legal authority should be suspended when you have primary authorities or stronger secondary authorities to cite.

Practice guides generally are written for one jurisdiction, so it is easier to find relevant law cited in them. But the mission of practice guides is to provide a background in the law and certain "how to" information about the practice area, not to provide an up to the minute account of the prevailing authorities in the area. Thus, they generally are not cited as secondary authority unless there is a drastic lack of other authority on the issue you are researching.

We did not include dictionaries in the heading above. This is because you should never hope to find a relevant case from your jurisdiction cited in the definition of any given legal word relating to the issues you are researching.

SOURCES OF SECONDARY AUTHORITY

FYI

Again, here we must address the tendency to conflate the "the books" with "secondary sources." By directing you to secondary sources, we are not necessarily directing you to print (versus on-line) resources. Secondary sources are generally accessible in both media. Rather, we are positing - and know from experience - that secondary sources (wherever you find them) often contain the key to solving your legal inquiry efficiently and effectively.

Treatises and Restatements

Treatises and restatements are both a secondary persuasive authority on the law itself and a case finding tool. Treatises and restatements of the law generally are written with a national scope of reference, so the authors borrow from the law of many jurisdictions to find, explain, and critique the most common principles of the law on any given legal topic. They will also point out notable exceptions and innovations in the law from the jurisdictions where they are found. Treatises and restatements cite authority in support of their 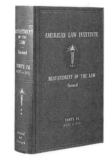 discussion of the law, so they are wonderful sources for primary persuasive authorities on the topics you are researching. Among these citations, you probably will find citations to one or more cases from your jurisdiction, but this is not enough to begin to exhaust the potentially controlling authorities on your issue.

The value of treatises to legal research is three-fold. First, as a source of background information in an area, they can be invaluable. Second, many treatises and all of the restatements of the law promulgated by the American Law Institute, although secondary authority, have iron-clad reputations leading to a very high persuasive value when used to support other authorities from your jurisdiction and elsewhere. You cannot contradict controlling authority with a treatise or restatement, but when the two agree, citing a treatise or restatement in support of your discussion is well worth the time and effort. Third, reference to treatises also is a useful check on your own formulation of the rules and elements of the rules on a given topic. When we check a restatement or major treatise and find a different rule stated than the one we have formulated on a given issue, we are given pause, and will go back and recheck our own primary authorities to make sure we have analyzed them correctly.

Law Review Articles and Legal Periodical Indices

Law review articles are an important secondary persuasive authority, and are excellent sources for primary persuasive authorities and other secondary authorities on the very particular topics that the articles discuss. Occasionally, they can be a useful tool for finding controlling authorities if the article focuses on the law in your jurisdiction. In most instances, however, law review articles will review the law from a variety of jurisdictions, and references to your jurisdiction's law will be hit or miss.

Westlaw and Lexis each provide access to law review articles. In print, an index to legal periodicals is used to locate law review articles and other publications that discuss your topic. These indices are organized by topic, which generally are key words, terms of art, and short phrases used in the articles themselves, and the indices present a listing of the titles and citations to the articles and publications.

SOURCES TO CHECK THE VIABILITY
OF YOUR AUTHORITIES

Shepard's Citations and KeyCite

KeyCite on Westlaw, and Shepard's on Lexis, are on-line resources that satisfy the need to check your authorities to make sure they have not been overruled or superseded or otherwise have become questionable as legal authority. (This process is described in detail in Chapter 4).

The primary *printed* sources to check the viability of your authorities are the various volumes and series of Shepard's Citations. Shepard's Citations volumes are organized by jurisdiction or subject matter, and within a given set of volumes, they list each case and certain other authorities issued or promulgated by that jurisdiction (or with that subject matter) and after each listing, they cite every case that has cited the authority. Furthermore, they code the citations to indicate which headnotes of the case were referenced in the citing authority, and whether the authority "treated" the opinion in some legally significant way (such as to overrule, reverse, question, criticize, or follow the opinion). Thus, you can look up the listing for your authority, and scan the citations to see if your authority has been reversed or criticized or has some other subsequent history that would be important to your analysis of the authority.

Use of the Shepard's *books* to check citations has largely gone out of vogue, and most law school and law firm libraries do not even keep these volumes up to date. We recognize that as a reality of the 21ˢᵗ century and thus are not going to spend time regaling you with our stories of updating the law "in the books." That said, there is nothing about checking citations that has gone out of vogue – you *must* make sure that the law that you cite is still applicable when you cite it.

Pocket Parts and Supplements

Most digests, ALRs, treatises, and other hardbound sources provide a means to keep the material in the volumes up to date, and thus, reliable. Pocket parts are often inserted into the back of the volumes, or supplemental softbound volumes or hardbound volumes are printed and shelved with the volumes. These updates report new developments in the law or additional sources of information that have been enacted or handed down since the publication of the main volume. Researchers always should check for pocket parts or supplemental volumes when performing research to make sure that the material they are looking at is current and accurate.

IV.   REACHING YOUR GOAL AND KNOWING WHEN YOU ARE FINISHED

Chapter 8 discusses the topic of research planning and determining when you have completed your research in greater depth than this section. At some point in your research, you will find that all of the new authorities you are finding are citing the authorities you already have found. At this point, the following criteria may be used to determine if you are finished with your research:

(1) If you have found several (3-5) controlling authorities that agree with each other as to the legal issue at hand, and they are recent enough in time not to give you pause (within the last thirty years for a highest court/highest controlling authority and ten years for an intermediate level appellate court/second highest controlling authority is a good rule of thumb here);

(2) If you also found several good persuasive authorities that support your controlling authorities, including a treatise or other secondary authority that supports your findings;

(3) If you have reconciled or distinguished all contrary controlling authorities and any important persuasive authorities; and

(4) If you do not have any nagging questions that you know should be answered before you move on to writing;

Then, most likely, you are finished.

This is only a rule of thumb. It is not going to hold true in every research problem you will encounter in law school or in actual practice. But having some guidelines is better than having none.

Chapter 2

Researching Statutes and Constitutions

The United States still recognizes itself as a Common Law, as opposed to a Civil Law jurisdiction, but the law of the United States increasingly is dominated by statutory law. Lawyers always should stop and consider whether the issue they are researching might be covered by a statute, and even when their instincts tell them it probably is not, it is a good idea to make a quick check anyway, because national (federal), state, county, and local legislatures are working hard to put more and more topics under statutory regulation.

Constitutional law touches many other areas of the law, and competent legal researchers will make sure that they have enough background knowledge of the area of law wherein their issues lie to recognize situations where federal or state constitutional law may play a role in the determination of the answers to the issues. The process of finding constitutional provisions is the same as finding statutory sections, but the interpretation of constitutional provisions often is more elaborate and may require consideration of a broader range of legal sources.

I.   ON-LINE RESEARCH FOR STATUTORY AND CONSTITUTIONAL LAW

A.   A comparison of free internet resources and Westlaw and Lexis

As discussed in Chapter 1, many resources exist on the internet to research statutes, especially if you have a good understanding of the structure and organization of the statutes you are researching and if you have a good understanding of what accurate results will look like when you find them. For example, if you already have knowledge that there is a statutory provision in the State of Illinois that governs dog bite liability, and if you already have a general idea of what this provision should provide and you will know it when you see it, it is fairly safe to use one of the free resources of the web to find that provision. (See <u>Illustration 2</u> below).

The problem with this approach for actual legal research on behalf of a client with even a simple legal problem is that most often you will *not know* whether and how many provisions might exist that would govern your issue, and even if you do know that some provisions exist, you may not know exactly what the titles or popular names of these provisions will be. You may not know what these provisions might look like ahead of time, and it is no sure bet that you or even an experienced researcher will know the correct sections when you see them. And in many situations, you will not know the structure and organization of the statutes well enough to know when you have exhausted the resource for applicable law. Add to this the fact that government or other freely searchable web sites may not be updated as frequently you would like them to be, and this should give you pause when you think about how much is riding on your getting completely accurate results for your clients and their delicate and potentially devastating legal problems. Not knowing the structure and organization of the statutes and being concerned about the accuracy and timeliness of free online resources will force you to search broadly and repetitively and wade through large numbers of results in order to compensate for the limitations of the free research. At best, this kind of inefficiency adds up to a great expense in terms of billable hours or simply expenditure of your limited time that more than surpasses the cost savings of using a free on-line resource. At worst, you flirt with malpractice because you may get out-of-date, inaccurate research results and use them to provide an incorrect, unreliable answer to the client or your boss.

FOOD FOR THOUGHT

What happens if you use free internet sources for all of your statutory research?

If you ignore the books and do not or cannot use Westlaw or Lexis, our prediction is that you will spend so many billable hours tracking down the correct statutory sections on free internet sites that you will start to drive clients away. The process of checking and rechecking internet sites to make sure you have found all of the applicable law is time-consuming. General internet statutory sources most often are not annotated, so you will have to replicate the process of finding regulatory and administrative law associated with the statutes, and case law applying and interpreting the statutory sections in books or through other, unconnected internet resources. This process, too, is time-consuming, but all of this is necessary if you are to avoid committing malpractice in your legal research.

As risky and inefficient internet resources can be, that is how marvelously efficient and exhaustive the fee-based services of Westlaw and Lexis are. With Westlaw or Lexis, you can craft logical, precise searches that can give you logical, precise results in small numbers, and you can be sure that the databases are as up to date as they can be. As discussed in Chapter 1 and Chapter 3, searches employing Boolean logic and other search specifications can zero in on results in carefully limited numbers that will save time to review and more accurately complete your research tasks. Westlaw and Lexis also will give you the assurance that you have looked at the correct, up-to-date sources and exhausted them so that your research results and the legal opinions you render based on that research are reliable and correct.

This kind of utility and efficiency comes at a high price, namely the search fees charged by Lexis and Westlaw first to your law office and then to your clients. The cost can be so high that some law offices and clients will reject the use of the fee-based services in favor of research using printed materials or the free resources of the internet. As a result, to be truly prepared for the practice of law, you must master the researching of all three sources when it comes to researching questions of statutory and constitutional law.

B.   Illustration 1 – searching using Westlaw or Lexis

The following illustration uses Westlaw as the search vehicle. Some of the names of databases and search functions would be different on Lexis, but the process illustrated is the same for both systems.

Referring back to the hunter's case in Chapter 1, the facts were: **A hunter with a rifle runs into someone's home in pursuit of a running deer and trips and falls and discharges his weapon injuring a housewife.**

From this, we derived several search terms:

Hunter, hunting, and negligence [party, action, potential claim for liability];

Weapons, guns, rifles and negligence with guns; weapons in household or indoors; accidental discharge of weapon;

accidental shooting [actions and items involved in the problem];

Trespassing and negligence while trespassing; liability for damage or injury to property owner [potential liabilities to a party]

These could be combined in many different ways taking advantage of synonyms and alternative phrasing for the concepts listed here. One example, using the Boolean logical relationship of "within the same sentence" (expressed in Westlaw as: **/s**) to connect our terms, would be:

hunter or hunting /s weapon or rifle or gun /s accident or accidental or negligent or negligence or injure or injuring or trespass or trespassing or trespasser

This could be shortened using the universal ending function (on Westlaw, it is: **!**). For example, using this ending on "hunt" would mean that "**hunt!**" as a search term will retrieve: hunt hunts hunter hunting and any other word with the first four letters "hunt." Also, on Westlaw, if you leave a space between words the system will assume that you mean the word "or" so that "**weapon rifle gun**" would be interpreted by Westlaw as "weapon or rifle or gun." (Lexis, on the other hand, asks for the word "or" to communicate the concept of "or"). We would then modify our search as follows:

hunt! /s weapon rifle gun /s accident! negligen! injur! trespass!

Having planned our first search query, we can turn to Westlaw. After logging in, the first screen will look something like this (depending on whether you choose default settings or do something more customized with your Westlaw account):

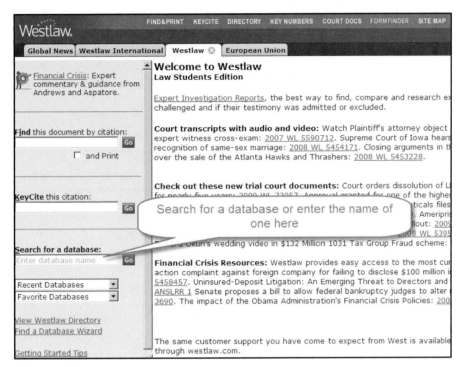

We have not discussed jurisdiction with our hunter problem. Assume for now that all of the events occurred in Louisiana and both parties (the hunter and the housewife) are Louisiana citizens. With this scenario, Louisiana law would apply, and we will want to look for Louisiana statutes.

On Westlaw, it is a simple matter to find the correct database within which to find your applicable statutes: you simply add the postal abbreviation of the state to the suffix "-ST" to pull up statutory sections without annotations (notes from cases that have applied the statute and other research aids), or add the suffix "-ST-ANN" to the state's postal abbreviation to pull up the statutes with annotations. If you select the statutes without annotations, then your search terms must appear in an actual section of the statutes, but if you select the annotated statutes, then your terms will pull up statutes containing the search terms or statutes whose annotations from cases and other authorities contain the search terms.

Assume for now that you are happy to pull up sections containing your search terms or sections with annotations containing your search terms. You would enter "LA-ST-ANN" in the database entry box indicated by the callout in the image above. The next screen you will see is a search screen:

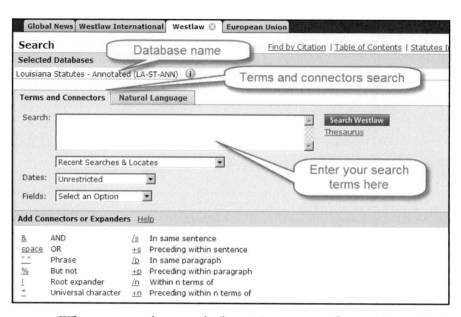

When we run that search (hunt! /s weapon rifle gun /s accident! negligen! injur! trespass!) in this database, we retrieve the following results screen:

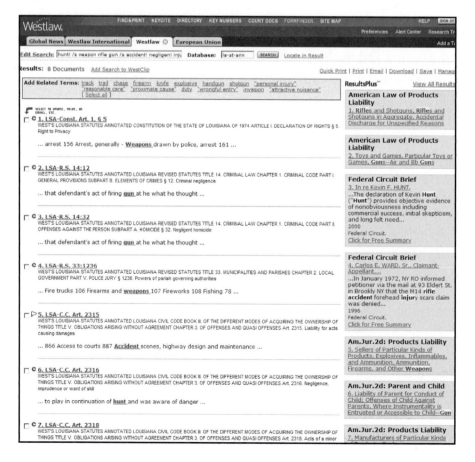

The results screen provides quite a bit of information. First, you can see that you pulled up eight sections whose terms or whose annotations contained your search terms. Second, on the left you will see a list of the sections you pulled up. The list contains the title and subtitles of each section, which will help to orient you within the results. For example, you can see that one of your results is a constitutional provision and several of them are criminal law provisions. The constitutional provision is on privacy, and does not seem to have anything to do with our situation. Furthermore, our problem dealt with civil liability of the hunter to the housewife, so a detour into the possible criminal law implications of our scenario most likely is not something the client will want to pay for. The list also shows a bit of the context around each of your terms. This should help you pick which of the eight sections you will want to look at first.

As you can see, there are a lot more results here than just a list of statutory sections. Westlaw provides other research aids—secondary sources such as treatises or encyclopedia (Am. Jur.) provisions, legal briefs from cases, and case finding resources from digests or annotated law reports—all of which the system calculates to be on point and therefore potentially useful to you based on your search query terms.

The sixth item on your list pertains to negligence and seems the most relevant. You can access that item by clicking on it (it is an active link). What you will see is the following:

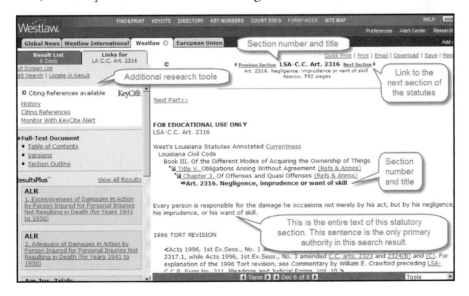

This screen reveals the small, one sentence text of the statute—this is, of course, the only part of this screen that contains primary, potentially controlling legal authority. Everything else on the screen is either a reference aid or a supplemental search tool.

We have indicated an important feature of the page here in the link at the top for the next section (and previous section) of this title of the Louisiana Civil Code. It is very important when researching statutes on-line to make use of these links and to search several sections before and after each of your "hits" from your search results. The reason for this is that related sections often are grouped together by those who draft or codify the statutes and several sections before or after your initial selection may be just as relevant to your research as the initial section you are viewing. Even if you are using an internet source other than Westlaw or Lexis, you should look for a link to the outline or table of contents of the entire title, chapter, or subdivision of the statutes where the section you are examining appears. Looking at an outline or table of contents often will reveal other sections of the statutes that also have a bearing on your issue. Whether the prior or subsequent sections are actively linked or not, you always should check ahead and behind your search results to see what else has been codified in the statutes on the same or a similar topic as the provision before you.

If you scroll down further in the left sidebar or the main window of this item you will see a host of additional search tools, not just the annotations from cases, but cross-references to any other potentially relevant areas of the statute, links to any administrative or regulatory law (the second form of primary, potentially controlling authority) associated with the statute, law review articles and other commentary, and many other secondary sources thought by the Westlaw system to be on point based on your search terms and the content of this statute. Eventually, you will get to the annotations themselves, including the one that triggered the hit because it contained your search terms:

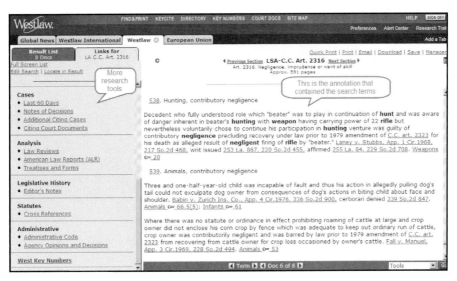

The results of this search provide a good starting point for your re-search, but we emphasize that this is only a starting point. You must look at or eliminate the other sections that your search pulled up. You might run other searches containing different search terms or a different mix of search terms. And you can follow up on the statutory research tools that Westlaw has offered to you in connection with this search and any others that you run. All of this effort is just to find statutes or constitutional provisions, and it remains for you to look at administrative law and cases and most likely to search for secondary authority, too.

C.   Illustration 2 – searching for statutory provisions using an internet source

As we mentioned above, free internet sources for statutes and con-stitutions are readily available but they have their limitations. The internet is great when you already know the statutory section that you want to find and you only want to pull up a copy of it. There is no risk and downside to that search method---you will either find it or you won't, and if you are familiar with the provision, you will know it when you find it.

For example, if in law school you learn that certain states have enacted "Dram Shop Acts" that impose liability on persons who provide alcohol to visibly intoxicated persons who then go out and injure other persons, and you want to check to see if Michigan has enacted such a statute, you can search on Google or another search engine for "Michigan statutes" and you will find the site http://www.legislature.mi.gov/;

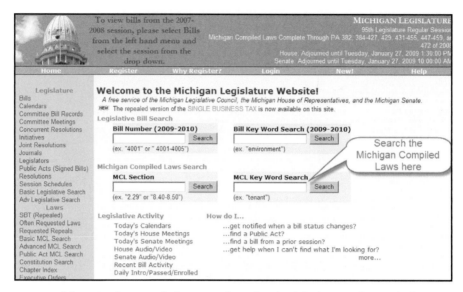

Here, in the search function box for the Michigan Compiled Laws, you can enter "dram shop act" and receive the following results:

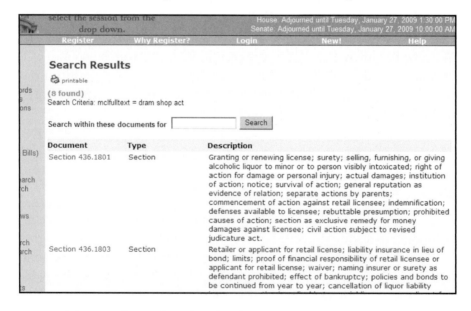

The search produced eight documents (statutory sections), and the first item in the results list looks promising. If you have a general familiarity with what "Dram Shop Acts" provide, then you should recognize that this most likely is Michigan's Dram Shop Act. Clicking on the link for the first item will allow you to check this out for yourself:

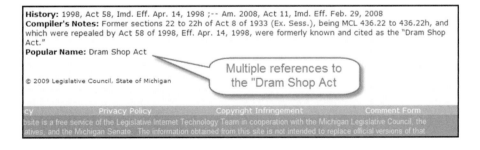

How did our search pull up this statute? Because Michigan used the popular name "Dram Shop Act" in connection with this statute, as revealed at the bottom of the section we have pulled up:

The problem is most legal research involves issues where you do know whether or how many statutory provisions exist that apply to your issues. You may not know what these provisions will be called, what title they will bear, or even a decent sounding popular name for the statutes. Your knowledge of the statutory law in the applicable area of law and the applicable jurisdiction may be so limited that you may not know that you have found the correct provisions when you pull them up on your screen. All of this points to the need to use other sources in print or on-line to complete the research task.

Returning to our research problem involving the hunter, we were curious to find out if Louisiana had statutory provisions that might regulate the situation of our hunter's accidental shooting and injuring of the housewife. If you search for "Louisiana statutes" on Google or another search you should find the site http://www.legis.louisiana.gov/lss/tsrs-search.htm.

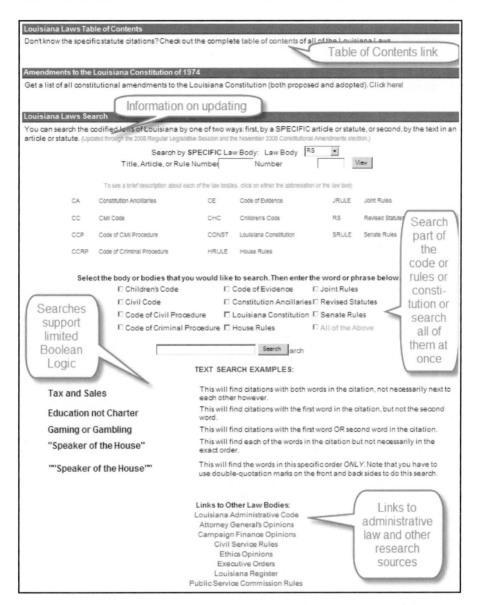

This site is useful. It allows you to search various parts of the code and the Louisiana Constitution. It even allows you to use a limited form of Boolean logic in your searches. Because of this, you can try to run a search query that is very close to the search we used on Westlaw:

(hunt or hunting or hunter) and (accident or accidental or negligent or negligence or injury) and (weapon or gun or rifle).

The query uses parentheses to try to replicate the connections of terms that we desire; in other words, we want one of several actions or actors to be present (hunt or hunting or hunter) but we also want one of several words to describe the occurrence (accident or accidental or negligent or negligence or injury). In this search for statutory sections that are on point, we will select the Civil Code and Revised Statutes rather than the constitution or other parts of the code and rules, and we will enter the search in the Search box because we do not know the title, Article, or Section Number of the laws that we are searching for.

Select the body or bodies that you would like to search. Then enter the word or phrase below.		
☐ Children's Code	☐ Code of Evidence	☐ Joint Rules
☑ Civil Code	☐ Constitution Ancillaries	☑ Revised Statutes
☐ Code of Civil Procedure	☐ Louisiana Constitution	☐ Senate Rules
☐ Code of Criminal Procedure	☐ House Rules	☐ All of the Above

(hunt or hunting or hunter) and (acc [Search] arch

The only problem is the system doesn't seem to like our search.

New Search

No documents matched your query. Click "New Search" to try again.

Previous | Next | New Search

The parentheticals most likely were the problem, but when you drop them, you lose the inherent logic of the search. If you search for **hunt or hunting or hunter and accident or accidental or negligent or negligence or injury and weapon or gun or rifle** you most likely will get a huge number of hits because what you asked for is "every document that has the word 'hunt' in it, or that has the word 'hunting' in it, or that has the word 'hunter' in it, and so on down the search string. If you run this search, this is what you will find:

Your query on hunt or hunting or hunter and accident or accidental or negligent or negligence or injury and weapon or gun or rifle found more than **200** documents. The first **200** will be listed in groups of **20**.

Previous | Next | New Search

1. RS 22:753 - **Policies under standard valuation law**
[Last Modified: 10/13/2008 10:37:54 PM]

2. RS 30:2063 - **Prevention of accidental releases**
[Last Modified: 01/01/2005 12:00:00 AM]

3. RS 40:1752 - **Handling of machine guns unlawful; exceptions**
[Last Modified: 01/01/2005 12:00:00 AM]

4. RS 56:104 - **License fees; reciprocity; exceptions**

This is not a good outcome because 200 sections (actually, the screen says "more than 200 documents") is a lot to go through. Compare this to the Westlaw results above (8 documents). It is doubtful that more than a handful of these sections will have anything to do with our issue.

Is there a way to narrow the results down? The only way is to narrow the search, and when your terms are only connected by "and" or "or" connectors, to narrow the search you have to drop out terms. For example, **hunting and negligence and weapon** or **hunter and negligent and gun** or **hunt and accident and rifle**. This may achieve the goal of limiting the numbers of the results but it will force you to run multiple searches to pick up the alternate terms that you derived that also represent your issue. Why? Because one or more limited searches might fail to pick up any documents but each additional search gives the opportunity to pick up additional documents. For example, if you run the first narrowed down search, **hunting and negligence and weapon**, you will find **no documents**. If you run the second search, **hunter and negligent and gun**, you will find **no documents**. If you run the third search, **hunt and accident and rifle**, you will find **no documents**. Finally, if you shorten the search to just **hunter and negligent** you will find two documents:

There are 2 documents that match your query on hunter and negligent .

Previous | Next | New Search

1. RS 9:2795.1 - Limitation of liability of farm animal activity sponsor or professional; exceptions; required warning
[*Last Modified: 01/01/2005 12:00:00 AM*]

2. RS 9:2795.3 - Limitation of liability of equine activity sponsor; exceptions; required warning
[*Last Modified: 09/08/2006 03:29:44 PM*]

Result Pages: 1

Previous | Next | New Search

Two documents is a good number, but these turn out to have nothing to do with our issue. Why did this happen? The problem is that the connection "and" or "or" within an entire document is a very loose connection. Any document with the word "hunter" appearing *somewhere* in the document and the word "negligent" appearing *somewhere* in the document gets pulled up. A tighter connection (hunter /3 negligent) would have a much better chance of pulling up relevant results, but that level of Boolean logic is not available on most free internet sites.

So, we find ourselves back at the drawing board. You can devise any number of short searches combining and recombining the terms until you finally pull up a statutory section or two that is on point. But at this point in your search, your incentive to keep going no doubt is fed by the knowledge that you did find at least one relevant section in your Westlaw search. In real life, if you intended to rely on the internet sources alone, you would never have run a Westlaw search, and if you never ran a Westlaw search, you might draw the conclusion from all of the searches we ran so far on this internet site that there simply is no statutory section having any impact on our problem under Louisiana law. That would be a logical conclusion, but it is one that we refuted easily by our earlier success on Westlaw. This set of circumstances should give you pause when you think about using the internet alone for legal research.

Because we are talking about hunting, we will point out that we have one last chance to find our quarry: the statutory table of contents. In this problem, this turns out to be a non-starter because the Louisiana Civil Code has 3,556 provisions that are only loosely grouped in sections with other provisions on a similar topic. The code is not organized into titles and chapters and sections. Thus, trying to browse through 3,556 separate provisions solely on the basis of their titles is a painful and time consuming process. It is a very thick forest within which our quarry hides.

II.   RESEARCHING STATUTORY AND CONSTITUTIONAL LAW IN PRINTED MATERIALS

There is a very acceptable and cost-efficient alternative to searching the internet for statutory and constitutional provisions: print resources. In many research situations, print resources can be used more efficiently and therefore more cheaply than fee-based on-line sources or internet sources. In particular, annotated statutes are organized and printed with the researcher in mind. The index to the annotated statutory compilation will identify and cross-reference statutory topics that will lead to all of the relevant statutory sections, and the sec-  tions themselves will provide references to regulatory and administrative law that also govern the issue at hand, case law applying and interpreting the statutory provision, and other search tools and secondary sources that will further help you to complete your research. As mentioned above, it often is easier to review the structure of a governing set of statutory law by reviewing the codification of the laws in print and flipping pages from one applicable section to the next. The decision to use or not to use print resources should never be made with a view that statutes are old-fashioned or out-dated; on the contrary, they are as lively, up-to-date, and useful in the twenty-first century as they ever have been.[1]

The process of researching printed sources is the same as using on-line sources. You must break down your issue into search terms—key words, concepts, and terms of art—that will enable you to find the correct legal topics and ultimately the correct statutory sections that will govern your issue. The difference is that you will then look these up in an index and follow the references and cross-references therein to locate the actual statutory sections that are on point.

A general index or descriptive word index will list topics alphabetically but the authors of the index will list a great variety of synonyms and alternate terms and cross-reference them to the terminology used in the statutory compilation you are researching. If you search "gun" or "rifle" for example, the index will point you to the topic of "weapons." The 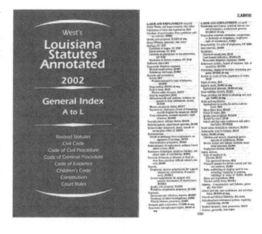 topical listing of "weapons" will point out a variety of sub-topics that you will scan until you find a sub-topic that points you to an actual statutory provision.

Once you have a provision to look up, an annotated statutory source will assist you with additional research tools (indicated by the arrows in the images on the next page):

---

1 "Print" sources need not actually be in print on paper. Most statutory compilations are available in CD-Rom format, so you might carry home the entire multi-volume set of the Code of Alabama in your purse or briefcase to work on over the weekend.

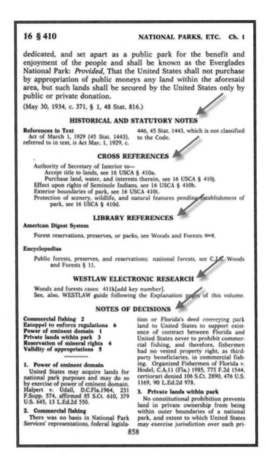

The **Historical and Statutory Notes** explain the history and development of this provision of law. The **Library References** lead you to secondary sources and other research tools. With other statutory sections, there may be a section devoted to law review and journal commentaries concerning the statute. The **Cross References** suggest other statutory sections or constitutional provisions that may also be on point on your issue based on the fact that you are looking at this statutory section. With other statutory sections there may be **Administrative Code References** or **Code of Regulation References** (e.g., with a federal statute, there may be citations to the Code of Federal Regulations, and with a state statute, there may be citations to the code of state regulations) providing citations to further rules and regulations that might govern your issue. The **Notes of Decisions** section presents annotations from case law applying and potentially interpreting this statutory section. All of this enables you to find the relevant sources for your issue as quickly and efficiently as possible.

III.   TIPS FOR RESEARCHING THE CONSTITUTION OF THE UNITED STATES OF AMERICA

We the people, in order to form a more perfect union . . . .

The United States Constitution is the foundation of the federal law in the United States and a regulator of state laws. The Constitution is a "living" document—meaning that the prevailing view of scholars of constitutional interpretation is that the U.S. Constitution is not a static text, but is meant to be interpreted and applied in light of current conditions in the country.

"Framers' Intent," a phrase referring to the interpretations, intentions, and aspirations of the drafters of the Constitution as to their work product, plays an important role in untangling thorny ambiguities in the text of the Constitution in a way not seen with ordinary legislation. People would rather pick the brain of James Madison than any 21st Century Supreme Court justice on the meaning and application of the Constitution.

The primary interpreter of the Constitution is the United States Supreme Court. This leads to some pretty heady case law. This area of the law gets very interesting, because the opinions of the Court are so detailed and complex, and the people writing them have such distinct personalities and persuasions. You often get multiple dissents and pluralities, and a jumble of opinions in cases that are hard to reconcile. The complex and high caliber problems of constitutional law attract some high-powered scholars, so the commentary written on the Constitution is as weighty and fruitful as the opinions that are the subject of this commentary.

A.   Primary print sources for researching and interpreting the constitution

Locating cases is a primary goal, and the usual suppliers (from West) lead you to them.

1.   United States Code Annotated, Constitution of the United States Annotated

These volumes are part of West's United States Code Annotated (U.S.C.A.). Each article, section, and clause of the Constitution is annotated in the Notes of Decisions section with every case  that cites the clause or section, cross-referenced to digest topics and encyclopedia sections. There also is a good index. (Remember West's promise: We'll be comprehensive so you can be, too.)

2.   United States Code Service, Constitution

The one-time competitor to West (Lawyers Cooperative) produced this volume, which also has annotations and a useful index. It also is cross-referenced to a lot of other former Lawyer's Cooperative products, such as ALRs.

3.   The Constitution of the United States of America (Library of Congress Edition)

The Congressional Research Service of the Library of Congress has put together a nice set of volumes with the text of each article, section, and clause, and it includes analysis and commentary by the editorial staff. In the commentary, important U.S. Supreme Court cases are cited and discussed, and references are made to the proceedings of the Constitutional Convention, and to various dissenting opinions of justices and other materials. Tables include:

- Proposed amendments pending before the states;

- Proposed amendments not ratified by the states (the Equal Rights Amendment, for example);

- Acts of Congress held unconstitutional in whole or in part;

- State constitutional provisions and state statutes held unconstitutional in whole or in part;

- Local ordinances held unconstitutional;

- U.S. Supreme Court decisions overruled by subsequent Supreme Court decisions.

This set is held to be a useful starting point for research into any constitutional law problem.

4.   Digests

Various digests exist to lead you to cases on constitutional law topics: U.S. Supreme Court Digest (West); Digest of the United States Supreme Court Reports, Lawyers Edition (LEXIS Law Pub.). The Federal Digest and Federal Practice Digest in its various editions (3rd, 4th etc.) include citations to U.S. Supreme Court cases.

5.   ALR annotations

A.L.R. Federal and A.L.R. 1st, 2nd, 3rd, 4th, and 5th series may contain law report annotations on constitutional law issues.

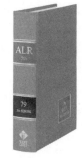

6.   Shepard's

United States Citations and state units cover cases citing and interpreting the Constitution.

B.   Secondary sources for federal constitutional interpretation

There are voluminous writings on every significant topic of constitutional law. This area attracts the best legal minds. In that this area of law is complex, and the opinions of the Supreme Court are highly complicated and often confusing from the multiple opinions, pluralities, concurrences, and so forth, and because it is widely believed that a proper interpretation includes reference to background and historical information from the framing of the Constitution, secondary persuasive sources are very important to this area, and they should be looked to more routinely than in other areas of the law.

1.   Collections of commentary and bibliographies

Constitutional law is rich in its collections of commentary and other secondary sources. *The Encyclopedia of the American Constitution* contains 2,100 articles collected for the Bicentennial. There also was some bibliographic collecting. *The Founder's Constitution* contains five volumes of documents that bear on the text and drafting of the Constitution. *A Comprehensive Bibliography of American Constitutional and Legal History, 1896-1979* is a multi-volume bibliography of resources, while *The Constitution of the United States: A Guide and Bibliography to Current Scholarly Research* is a good one volume work collecting authorities. The *Constitutional Law Dictionary* is more than a dictionary, it collects cases, too.

2.   Leading treatises on constitutional law

The following are generally considered to be highly authoritative works on constitutional law issues: Ronald Rotunda and John Nowak's *Treatise on Constitutional Law: Substance and Procedure*; Laurence Tribe's one volume *American Constitutional Law*; Chester Antieau's *Modern Constitutional Law*. Naturally, if your constitutional law professor has other favorites, or criticizes one or more of these authors, follow your professor's guidance while in her course.

3.   Framers' intent (and the founding fathers' information)

It can be a chore to find and interpret the source material for framers' intent, but the following volumes can help: *Documents Illustrative of the Formation of the Union of the American States* (Library of Congress Leg. Ref. Serv.); *Documentary History of the Constitution of the United States of America, 1786-1870* (Library of Congress Leg. Ref. Serv.); *The Federalist*—essays and papers of some of the primary drafters, Madison, Jay, and Hamilton. Sometimes referred to as the Federalist Papers. Some of these resources are on-line—Westlaw's BICENT database contains the above three sources (note that your student Westlaw license may not allow you access to this database) and you also can run searches in Westlaw's LH-1776 database that contains historical sources and documents from the time period of the founding of the nation, including the Federalist papers, the debates in the federal convention of 1787 (as recorded by James Madison), the Declaration of Independence, and the Articles of Confederation.

4.   The Constitutional Convention

If you find a need to look at the actual debates and proceedings of the Constitutional Convention, try the following: *Records of the Federal Constitution of 1787*; Elliot's Debates (*The Debates, Resolutions, and Other Proceedings in Convention, on the Adoption of the Federal Constitution* (1827)); *Documentary History of the Ratification of the Constitution*, or Westlaw's LH-1776 database described in the section above.

IV.   TIPS FOR RESEARCHING STATE CONSTITUTIONS

The official version of a state constitution generally is printed in the state's official statutes. West and a few others will print annotations to the state constitution in their annotated version of the state statutes. A state's constitution generally will be accessible from any internet site containing the state's statutes. Westlaw or Lexis will access a state's constitution from the state's statutory databases (on Westlaw, the database will be the state's postal abbreviation followed by the suffix **–ST** or **–ST-ANN**; e.g., SD-ST-ANN for South Dakota Codified Laws Annotated).

Columbia University School of Law's Legislative Drafting Research Fund has collected texts of the 50 state constitutions in the *Constitutions of the United States: National and State* volumes. This also has a companion set of volumes called *Index Digest of State Constitutions*, which reports the various constitutional provisions from the states on a collection of topics for comparative purposes. *State Constitutional Conventions, Commissions and Amendments* (microfiche collection) gathers documents and information from the conventions that established the state constitutions.

V. TIPS FOR RESEARCHING FEDERAL STATUTORY LAW

A. How federal laws are made

"All Legislative Powers herein granted shall be vested in a Congress of the United States, which shall consist of a Senate and House of Representatives."

U.S. Const. art. I, § 1.

When researching statutory law, it will be beneficial to understand how the laws are made. This section answers the questions of when and how a bill become a law, a primary legal authority, and what is the difference between the statutes passed by a legislature and the code of laws that are organized to allow easier access to the laws that govern our day to day legal issues.

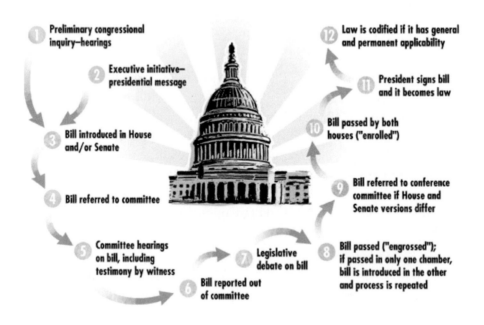

1.   Forms of congressional action[2]

The work of Congress is initiated by the introduction of a proposal in one of four principal forms: the bill, the joint resolution, the concurrent resolution, and the simple resolution. A worthwhile resource to familiarize yourself with now is http://thomas.loc.gov/, which is the Library of Congress's compilation of legislative information in a relatively easy-to-search format.

a.   Bills

A bill is the form used for most legislation, whether permanent or temporary, general or special, public or private. A bill originating in the House of Representatives is designated by the letters "H.R.," signifying "House of Representatives," followed by a number that it retains throughout all its parliamentary stages. Bills introduced in the Senate get an "S.," followed by a number. Bills are presented to the President for action when approved in identical form by both the House of Representatives and the Senate.

b.   Joint resolutions

Joint resolutions may originate either in the House of Representatives or in the Senate. There is little practical difference between a bill and a joint resolution. Both are subject to the same procedure, except for a joint resolution proposing an amendment to the Constitution. On approval of such a resolution by two-thirds of both the House and Senate, it is sent directly to the Administrator of General Services for submission to the individual states for ratification. It is not presented to the President for approval. A joint resolution originating in the House of Representatives is designated "H.J.Res.," followed by its individual number. Joint resolutions become law in the same manner as bills.

---

2 This section is largely drawn from the U.S. House of Representative Information Resources, and the publication "How Our Laws Are Made," reported at http://thomas.loc.gov/home/lawsmade.toc.html (last visited Sept. 10, 2008).

c.   Concurrent resolutions

Matters affecting the operations of both the House of Representatives and Senate are usually initiated by means of concurrent resolutions. A concurrent resolution originating in the House of Representatives is designated "H.Con.Res.," followed by its individual number. On approval by both the House of Representatives and Senate, they are signed by the Clerk of the House and the Secretary of the Senate. They are not presented to the president for action.

d.   Simple resolutions

A matter concerning the operation of either the House of Representatives or Senate alone is initiated by a simple resolution. A resolution affecting the House of Representatives is designated "H.Res.," followed by its number. They are not presented to the President for action.

2.   Introduction and referral to committee

Any Member in the House of Representatives may introduce a bill at any time while the House is in session by simply placing it in the "hopper" provided for this purpose at the side of the Clerk's desk in the House Chamber. The sponsor's signature must appear on the bill. A public bill may have an unlimited number of co-sponsoring Members. The bill is assigned its legislative number by the Clerk and referred to the appropriate committee by the Speaker, with the assistance of the Parliamentarian. The bill is then printed in its introduced form, which you can read in Bill Text. If a bill was introduced today, summary information about it can be found in Bill Status Today.

An important phase of the legislative process is the action taken by committees. It is during committee action that the most intense consideration is given to the proposed measures; this is also the time when the people are given their opportunity to be heard. Each piece of legislation is referred to the committee that has jurisdiction over the area affected by the measure.

3.   Consideration by committee—public hearings and markup sessions

Usually the first step in this process is a public hearing, where the committee members hear witnesses representing various viewpoints on the measure. Each committee makes public the date, place, and subject of any hearing it conducts. The Committee Meetings scheduled for today are available along with other House Schedules. Public announcements are also published in the Daily Digest portion of the Congressional Record.

A transcript of the testimony taken at a hearing is made available for inspection in the committee office, and frequently the complete transcript is printed and distributed by the committee.

After hearings are completed, the bill is considered in a session that is popularly known as the "mark-up" session. Members of the committee study the viewpoints presented in detail. Amendments may be offered to the bill, and the committee members vote to accept or reject these changes.

This process can take place at either the subcommittee level or the full committee level, or at both. Hearings and markup sessions are status steps noted in the Legislative Action portion of Bill Status.

4.   Committee action

At the conclusion of deliberation, a vote of committee or subcommittee members is taken to determine what action to take on the measure. It can be reported, with or without amendment, or tabled, which means no further action on it will occur. If the committee has approved extensive amendments, they may decide to report a new bill incorporating all the amendments. This is known as a "clean bill," which will have a new number. Votes in committee can be found in Committee Votes.

If the committee votes to report a bill, the Committee Report is written. This report describes the purpose and scope of the measure and the reasons for recommended approval. House Report numbers are prefixed with "H. Rep." and then a number indicating the Congress (for example, H. Rep. 105-279, referring to a House Report from the 105th

Congress).

5.   House floor consideration

Consideration of a measure by the full House can be a simple or very complex operation. In general, a measure is ready for consideration by the full House after it has been reported by a committee. Under certain circumstances, it may be brought to the floor directly. The consideration of a measure may be governed by a "rule." A rule is itself a simple resolution, which must be passed by the House, that sets out the particulars of debate for a specific bill—how much time will allowed for debate, whether amendments can be offered, and other matters. Debate time for a measure is normally divided between proponents and opponents. Each side yields time to those Members who wish to speak on the bill. When amendments are offered, these are also debated and voted upon. If the House is in session today, you can see a summary of Current House Floor Proceedings. After all debate is concluded and amendments decided upon, the House is ready to vote on final passage. In some cases, a vote to "recommit" the bill to committee is requested. This is usually an effort by opponents to change some portion or to table the measure. If the attempt to recommit fails, a vote on final passage is ordered.

6.   Resolving differences

After a measure passes in the House, it goes to the Senate for consideration. A bill must pass both bodies in the same form before it can be presented to the President for signature into law. If the Senate changes the language of the measure, it must return to the House for concurrence or additional changes. This back-and-forth negotiation may occur on the House floor, with the House accepting or rejecting Senate amendments or the complete Senate text. Often a conference committee will be appointed with both House and Senate members. This group will resolve the differences in committee and report the identical measure back to both bodies for a vote. Conference committees also issue reports outlining the final version of the bill.

7.   Final steps

When either house orders the third reading of a bill, it simultaneously orders the **engrossment** of the bill. This is a formal reprinting of the bill in the final form that the bill will take before voting takes place in each chamber. (In earlier days, the final version was written up in large script, hence the term "engrossment.")

Votes on final passage, as well as all other votes in the House, may be taken by the electronic voting system which registers each individual Member's response. These votes are referred to as Yea/Nay votes or recorded votes, and are available in House Votes by Bill number, roll call vote number, or words describing the reason for the vote. Votes in the House may also be by voice vote, and no record of individual responses is available. After a measure has been passed in identical form by both the House and Senate, it is considered **"enrolled,"** and the **enrolled version** of the bill represents the official legislative enactment of the bill.

Presentation occurs when the enrolled version of the bill is sent to the President, who may sign the measure into law, veto it and return it to Congress, let it become law without signature, or, at the end of a session, pocket-veto it.

B.   Publication of federal laws[3]

One of the important steps in the enactment of a valid law is the requirement that it shall be made known to the people who are to be bound by it. If the President approves a bill, or allows it to become law without signing it, the original enrolled bill is sent from the White House to the Archivist of the United States for publication. If a bill is passed by both houses of Congress over the objections of the President, the body that last overrides the veto transmits it. It is then assigned a public law number, and paginated for the Statutes at Large volume covering that session of Congress.

The public and private law numbers run in sequence starting anew at the beginning of each Congress and, since 1957, they have been prefixed for ready identification by the number of the Congress. For example, the first public law of the 105th Congress is designated Public Law 105-1 and the first private law of the 105th Congress is designated Private Law

---

3   This section is drawn from the U.S. House of Representatives Information Resources, http://thomas.loc.gov/home/lawsmade.bysec/publication.html (last visited Sept. 10, 2008).

105-1. Subsequent laws of this Congress also will contain the same prefix designator—the second public law passed by the 105th Congress is designated Public Law 105-2, and so on.

1.   Slip laws

The first official publication of the statute is in the form generally known as the "slip law." In this form, each law is published separately as an unbound pamphlet. The heading indicates the public or private law number, the date of approval, and the bill number. The heading of a slip law for a public law also indicates the United States Statutes at Large citation. If the statute has been passed over the veto of the President, or has become law without the President's signature because he did not return it with objections, an appropriate statement is inserted instead of the usual notation of approval.

The Office of the Federal Register, National Archives and Records Administration prepares the slip laws and provides marginal editorial notes giving the citations to laws mentioned in the text and other explanatory details. The marginal notes also give the United States Code classifications, enabling the reader immediately to determine where the statute will appear in the Code. Each slip law also includes an informative guide to the legislative history of the law consisting of the committee report number, the name of the committee in each house, as well as the date of consideration and passage in each house, with a reference to the Congressional Record by volume, year, and date. A reference to presidential statements relating to the approval of a bill or the veto of a bill when the veto was overridden and the bill becomes law is included in the legislative history as a citation to the Weekly Compilation of Presidential Documents.

Copies of the slip laws are delivered to the document rooms of both houses where they are available to officials and the public. They may also be obtained by annual subscription or individual purchase from the Government Printing Office and are available in electronic form for computer access. Section 113 of title 1 of the United States Code provides that slip laws are competent evidence in all the federal and state courts, tribunals, and public offices.

2.   Statutes at Large

The United States Statutes at Large, prepared by the Office of the Federal Register, National Archives and Records Administration, provide a permanent collection of the laws of each session of Congress in bound volumes. Each volume contains a complete index and a table of contents. The volumes from 1956 through 1976 each contain a table of earlier laws affected. These tables were cumulated for 1956-1970 and supplemented for 1971-1975 in pamphlet form and discontinued in 1976. The 1963 through 1974 volumes also contain a most useful table showing the legislative history of each law in the volume. This latter table was not included in subsequent volumes because the legislative histories have appeared at the end of each law since 1975. There are also extensive marginal notes referring to laws in earlier volumes and to earlier and later matters in the same volume.

Under the provisions of a statute originally enacted in 1895, the version of the laws printed in the Statutes at Large is **legal evidence** of the terms and requirements of federal statutory law and will be accepted as **proof positive** of those laws in any court in the United States.

The Statutes at Large are a chronological arrangement of the laws exactly as they have been enacted. The fifth law passed by a Congress is printed immediately before the sixth law passed, regardless of the content of these laws. There is no attempt to arrange the laws according to their subject matter or to show the present status of an earlier law that has been amended on one or more occasions. The code of laws serves that purpose.

3.   United States Code

The United States Code contains a consolidation and codification of the general and permanent laws of the United States arranged according to subject matter under 50 Title headings (*see below*). It sets out the current status of the laws, as amended, without repeating all the language of the amendatory acts except where necessary for that purpose. The Code is declared to be **prima facie** evidence of those laws, meaning that the words viewed in the U.S. Code are held to be the terms of the law unless someone comes forward to rebut the U.S. Code version by reference to the Statutes at Large or the Slip Law version of the law. Its purpose is to present the laws in a concise and usable form without requiring recourse to the many volumes of the Statutes at Large containing the individual amendments.

The Code is prepared by the Law Revision Counsel of the House of Representatives. New editions are published every six years and cumulative supplements are published after the conclusion of each regular session of the Congress. The Code is also available in electronic form for computer access.

Twenty-two of the 50 titles have been revised and enacted into positive law, and two have been eliminated by consolidation with other titles. Titles that have been revised and enacted into positive law are referred to as **codified reenactments**, and they achieve the same status as the laws printed in the Statutes at Large; in other words, the U.S. Code text of a codified reenactment is legal evidence of the law and the courts will receive the text as proof positive of the terms of those laws. Eventually, all the titles will be revised and enacted into positive law. At that point, they will be updated by direct amendment.

4.   The 50 Titles of the United States Code

The Code is divided into 50 titles by subject matter. Each title is divided into sections. Sections within a title may be grouped together as subtitles, chapters, subchapters, parts, subparts, or divisions. Titles may also have appendices which may be divided into sections, rules, or forms.

The subjects covered by the 50 titles of the U.S. Code[4] are:

1.   General Provisions

2.   The Congress

3.   The President

4.   Flag and Seal, Seat of Government, and the States

5.   Government Organization and Employees

---

4 Law Revision Counsel, U.S. House of Representatives, http://uscode.house.gov/ (last visited Sept. 10, 2008).

6. Surety Bonds (repealed by the enactment of Title 31)

7. Agriculture

8. Aliens and Nationality

9. Arbitration

10. Armed Forces

11. Bankruptcy

12. Banks and Banking

13. Census

14. Coast Guard

15. Commerce and Trade

16. Conservation

17. Copyrights

18. Crimes and Criminal Procedure

19. Customs Duties

20. Education

21. Food and Drugs

22. Foreign Relations and Intercourse

23. Highways

24. Hospitals and Asylums

25. Indians

26. Internal Revenue Code

27. Intoxicating Liquors

28. Judiciary and Judicial Procedure

29. Labor

30. Mineral Lands and Mining

31. Money and Finance

32.   National Guard

33.   Navigation and Navigable Waters

34.   Navy (eliminated by the enactment of Title 10)

35.   Patents

36.   Patriotic Societies and Observations

37.   Pay and Allowances of the Uniformed Services

38.   Veterans' Benefits

39.   Postal Service

40.   Public Buildings, Property, and Works

41.   Public Contracts

42.   The Public Health and Welfare

43.   Public Lands

44.   Public Printing and Documents

45.   Railroads

46.   Shipping

47.   Telegraphs, Telephones, and Radiotelegraphs

48.   Territories and Insular Possessions

49.   Transportation

50.   War and National Defense

C.   Primary print sources for federal statutes

1.   United States Statutes at Large

The Statutes at Large has the exact language and form passed by Congress, and so it is the <u>official</u> law of the land. If other versions (other codifications) differ, they are in error and the Statutes at Large control. The Statutes at Large has three main parts: Public Laws, Private Laws, and Treaties.

a. Public laws

Public laws are the most important to this course of study and to your future research (until you get into an area where treaties are equally important, such as international law or intellectual property law). Public laws are further codified into the United States Code (U.S.C.) and commercial codifications, such as the United States Code Annotated by West (U.S.C.A.), and the United States Code Service (West, formerly Lawyers Cooperative) (U.S.C.S.). Public Laws are applicable to everyone in the U.S.A. They are referenced as:

P.L. 95-123 or Pub. L. 95-123.

As discussed above, this reference represents the "123rd" public law enacted by the 95th Congress, and it will be found in numerical (and thus chronological) order within the Statutes at Large, first by the Congress (95th) and then by the sequential enactment number (123). P.L. 95-123 follows P.L. 95-122 and precedes P.L. 95-124.

The Statutes at Large are cited as "Stat." e.g., 92 Stat. 1020. ***This is the official citation form*** for the Statutes at Large and the laws found therein, although when researching, either the Public Law number (P.L.) or the Statutes at Large (Stat.) citation will enable you to locate Public Laws in the Statutes at Large.

b. Private laws

Private Laws affect only single individuals or small groups, mainly in the areas of: (1) immigration and naturalization; and (2) personal claims involving the government, e.g., regarding the timeliness of a Tort Claims action against the United States. If Congress determined to make a U.S. citizen of Winston Churchill or a Cuban refugee such as Elian Gonzales, they would do it by passing a private law.

c.   Treaties

Treaties have the same importance and legal effect as the laws passed by Congress according to the U.S. Const. art. VI, cl. 2 (". . . all Treaties made, or which shall be made, under the Authority of the United States, shall be the supreme Law of the Land . . .") although they do not require the approval of the House of Representatives. Article II, § 2, cl. 2 of the United States Constitution gives the President the power, "with the Advice and Consent of the Senate," to make treaties, if approved by a two-thirds majority of the Senate quorum voting. In addition to the Statutes at Large, treaties are found in several reporter series, such as United States Treaties (U.S.T.), and Treaties and other International Acts Series (T.I.A.S.).

2.   Early publication of new laws and amendments to existing laws

The Statutes at Large and the United States Code both are published by the Government Printing Office. Thus, they are three to five years (Stat.) and twelve to twenty-four months (U.S.C.) behind the date of enactment of the laws they publish. There is also a delay with the two commercial services, U.S.C.S. and U.S.C.A., although it is only a few weeks delay in most instances.

a.   U.S.C.C.A.N.

When you need more timely information, West publishes the United States Code, Congressional & Administrative News (U.S.C.C.A.N.), an unofficial news publication. It is a respected source, but it is not an official source of the law—cite to it only when the law or amendment is not yet reported in one of the commercial services, U.S.C.A. or U.S.C.S. U.S.C.C.A.N. does not publish every law or amendment, only the more prominent and important ones (often the ones you will be looking for), and it gets them to press quicker than the other services. (U.S.C.C.A.N. also is a source of legislative history, which is discussed in the next chapter).

b.   U.S.C.S. Advance Service

There is a companion service to the U.S.C.S., the United States

Code Service Advance Service, which tries to get out new legislation within two to three weeks of passage. They use the Public Law Number for organization and issue a paper bound supplement.

c. Slip Laws, U.S. Law Week, Westlaw, and Lexis

The fastest print publication is by Slip Laws, although done by the Government Printing Office, they are distributed to subscribers such as law libraries within days or a week or so of passage. U.S. Law Week (U.S.L.W.) also gets to print quickly, although only the most important or controversial acts (cutting edge, newsworthy, etc.) are published here.

Fastest of all is Westlaw and Lexis, which contain databases for tracking proposed legislation and providing the text of each draft version as it progresses through the legislative process. Thus, if a bill becomes law, the final version immediately is available. Note, however, that because of the ability to track each version as it progresses, any search you run will pull up multiple versions of the same bill. What you are looking for is the official version passed by both houses, which is referred to as the **"enrolled" version**.

D. Codifications and subject organization

The Statutes at Large are chronological—a law is passed and printed in the volume for the 95th Congress; the 96th Congress amends it—the amendment shows up in the volume for that Congress. Other laws were passed on the same topic by the 88th, 90th, 91st and 93rd Congresses—these laws are found in the volumes for those Congresses. Nothing in the Statutes at Large cross-references or compiles the ongoing results of all this legislation. This is where the codification services enter the picture.

1. United States Code

Upon enactment, Public Laws are sent to the Congressional Office of Law Revision Counsel, who breaks the law down into its component parts and assigns the parts to the fifty titles and subsections of the U.S. Code.

While the Statutes at Large represents the official version of the laws actually voted upon and passed by the Congress, the U.S.C. is held to be "presumptively" official because it is a reorganization of the official version. Thus, the U.S.C. is presumed to be a correct statement of the law and may be cited. However, if there exists a difference between the Code and the Statutes at Large, the Statutes at Large controls and must be cited. Accordingly, the U.S.C. must be used with caution, and where a U.S.C. provision's express wording is crucial to your case or legal analysis, the prudent lawyer will always confirm that wording in the Statutes at Large.

However, if the title of the U.S. Code you are looking at is marked with an asterisk (*), this indicates that Congress has passed into positive law the "codified" versions of the law as found in the United States Code. Thus, the codified version in the U.S. Code is no longer simply presumptively correct, it becomes the <u>official</u> version, and the Statutes at Large version no longer controls (or, more accurately, the codified re-enactment takes its place among the Statutes at Large, thereby supplanting the original enactment). This has been done to 22 titles of the U.S. Code. So pay attention to asterisks! Note, however, that subsequent amendments to the codified re-enactments printed in the U.S. Code are simply "presumptively correct" even though they are printed in the same volume of the U.S. Code as the official text—that is, until Congress goes ahead and re-enacts the codified amendments into positive law.

The United States Code began in 1926 and is re-issued every six (6) years. It is updated by supplements during intervening years. It contains only the law, historical notes, and commentaries on the law.

2.   West's United States Code Annotated

West's United States Code Annotated ("U.S.C.A.") is organized exactly like and uses the same referencing system as the United States Code; <u>e.g.</u>, 17 U.S.C. § 101 (the U.S. Code version), is  found in the U.S.C.A. at 17 U.S.C.A. § 101. U.S.C.A. prints the same text (you hope), historical notes and commentaries found in the U.S.C.

itself, along with additional information added by West editors; e.g., law review references, C.F.R. elaboration, and annotations—brief quotes from and abstracts of cases that cite the statutory section at hand, which can help you find relevant cases that construe and apply the statute. West prints an annotation for *every* case that mentions a U.S. Code provision, so many of the cases will be redundant (they all say the same thing), but you can expect comprehensive coverage, and easily can skip to your jurisdiction's cases in the list of annotations. Annotations are subdivided by specific issues and topics from the area of law of the statutory section you are researching.

Special volumes annotate the United States Constitution, and the entire U.S.C.A. has a thorough index, including a "Popular Names Table," which references codified enactments by their "short titles." It has annual "pocket parts" to keep it current.

The U.S.C.A.'s main shortcoming is that is relies on the language of the U.S.C. itself, and the U.S.C. is only presumptively correct. If the U.S.C. codifiers commit "sins of omission and commission," West will replicate these errors. (Of course, West's typesetters and editors can make transcription errors of their own, too). Sometimes the U.S.C.A. will note an error in the language from the "official version," or annotations from cases will note an error, but this is not always the case.

The Bluebook requires citation to the U.S. Code (U.S.C.) for the codified version of a federal statute, not the U.S.C.A. If the U.S. Code is inconsistent with the Statutes at Large, citation must be to the Statutes at Large.

3.   United States Code Service

In the same manner as the U.S.C.A., the United States Code Service ("U.S.C.S.") prints the law so as to be consistent with the U.S. Code, so if you want to find 17 U.S.C. § 101 in the U.S.C.S. you look for 17 U.S.C.S. § 101. The U.S.C.S. includes everything that is in the U.S.C., plus law review and C.F.R. references (not necessarily the same ones found

in U.S.C.A.), and "annotations" referencing case law construing each code
provision. There is a General Index and
Popular Names Table, and the volumes
are kept current with pocket parts.

There are two differences between the U.S.C.A. and the U.S.C.S.:
before creating annotations, the pub-
lisher of U.S.C.S. tries to weed out inapposite, redundant, and irrelevant
cases that happen to cite the code. As a result, there usually are fewer
case references in the U.S.C.S. than in the U.S.C.A., but you suppos-
edly receive greater assurance of their relevance. If you trust the editors'
discretion, you might zero in on truly relevant cases more quickly with
U.S.C.S., but if you want to see the universe of cases citing the statute,
stick to U.S.C.A. Time might make that decision for you.

A second, very important difference between U.S.C.S. and
U.S.C.A. is that U.S.C.S. does not follow the U.S.C.'s wording. Instead,
U.S.C.S. editors check its wording against the Statutes at Large and, to
the extent a deviation is found, they include the official wording and highlight that passage, bringing it to the researcher's attention.

The United States Code Service includes other features that assist
legal researchers. Following the U.S.C.S.'s general presentation and general index, U.S.C.S. offers separate annotated renditions of the Federal
Rules of Civil Procedure, Criminal Procedure, Appellate Procedure, Administrative Procedure, U.S. Supreme Court Rules & Procedure, Federal
Circuit Court Local Rules, Federal Sentencing Guidelines, and others.
On the topic of regulatory law, the U.S.C.S. has an "Index & Finding
Aids to Code and Federal Regulations," which cross-references U.S.C.S.
provisions and the C.F.R. rules and regulations promulgated from the
statutory provision, and vice versa—you can move from the statute to the
regulatory law or from the regulatory law back to the statute.

VI.   TIPS FOR RESEARCHING STATE AND MUNICIPAL LEGISLATION

A.   Session laws

In the same manner as the federal government, state legislatures enact laws that are published in chronological order (in order of the date of passage of the laws) in volumes identified by the session of the legislature wherein the law was passed (akin to the U.S. Statutes at Large). Hence the term "Session Laws."

B.   Codifications of state laws

In that a yearly or bi-yearly report of the statutes passed in the chronological order of passage is not very useful to the researcher for finding all of the laws on a given topic, states codify their statutes in volumes referred to as the state **code** or **laws** or **statutes**, often with a descriptive reference such as **compiled**, **revised**, or **consolidated**. E.g., Missouri Revised Statutes; Illinois Compiled Statutes; Idaho Official Code; General Statutes of Connecticut; General Laws of the Commonwealth of Massachusetts.

The codes generally provide:

- Text of the state constitution (and sometimes the federal constitution);

- Text of the statutes themselves in the "proper" codified subject matter area;

- Historical notes (including a list of prior enactments of law on the same topic);

- Indices (to find the laws you should be looking at);

- Official commentary on the statute or the section at hand (this is unusual);

- Tables for referencing rules, administrative law relationships, cross-references to related sections and statutes, bill numbers that became session laws, popular names of legislation, etc. (this is common, and very useful);

- Court rules (the Mississippi Rules of Civil Procedure, etc.)

The official laws of the state are updated in the ordinary ways with pocket parts or pamphlets, supplements (often soft-bound), and replacement volumes.

C.   Annotated statutes

The usefulness of annotations to cases that carry out, interpret, or construe the statutes is not lost on the states (and West Publishing). You will find an annotated version of each state's laws. Sometimes the annotated version is the "official" version (or the only version) of the state statutes (e.g., New York), so check the Bluebook. Pocket-parts, pamphlets, and supplements are the preferred methods for updating annotated statutes.

D.   On-line services

Westlaw and Lexis are sources for each state's unannotated *or* official statutes (e.g., CA-ST on Westlaw), and almost all states' annotated statutes (e.g., CA-ST-ANN on Westlaw). Recent session laws for several states also can be found on Westlaw and Lexis. Indeed, these will be the most up-to-date versions of the statutes and session laws available. Note that the unannotated library will not necessarily be the "official" statutes. Many times on Westlaw, the xx-ST database does not get you the official state statutes—it gets you the text of the statutes as printed in one of West's annotated versions of the state statutes, but Westlaw withholds showing you the annotations. If you simply hate to read annotations, there you go.

If you want the official statutes, many states have a web site where you can access their official state statutes and sometimes their recent session laws. State bar associations often duplicate this service providing the same information and other links to state legislative material.

E.   Multiple states sources

Often, you will have the most success finding the statutory laws of multiple jurisdictions (or all 50 states) on a given subject in a topical publication of the loose-leaf variety, brought to you by private publishers such as Bureau of National Affairs (BNA), Commerce Clearing House (CCH), and others. For instance, if you want the laws of all fifty states on securities fraud (similar to federal Rule 10b-5), you could check out one of CCH's volumes on Blue Sky Law (the term coined for state securities laws), or Securities Litigation. If you want multiple states' laws on sexual harassment in the workplace, you could check out one of BNA's volumes on employment discrimination.

F.   Municipal law

A local public library or local law library most likely is the best or only place to look for local ordinances. Finding city codes or even publications of local ordinances on-line often is a hit or miss process, but some of you may be lucky enough to live (or study, or both) in a city that has reported its information on the Internet. For example, the St. Louis Public Library has created a searchable web site for the City of St. Louis Charter, Revised Code, Ordinances (starting in 1991), and even Alderman Meeting minutes (i.e., legislative history) starting in May 1998 (the library probably has paper copies of earlier minutes available for examination, but not on-line), all at the SL Public Library web site: www.slpl.lib.mo.us/cco/index.htm.

Finding cases that interpret these laws is even harder. You always can search on Westlaw or Lexis in a general state law database for the hits on the terms or the reference number/citation of a local ordinance. But very few "annotated" municipal codes exist. State digests sometimes devote attention to cases that interpret a municipal charter or local ordinance. You can search the annual index to the volumes, or search on-line (if the state digest is on-line).

Shepard's State Citations tracks cases that interpret municipal laws. There is a separate set of volumes called Shepard's Ordinance Law Annotations that annotate cases that construe municipal ordinances on broadly defined topics and specifically defined sub-topics from any number of jurisdictions (cities). Thus, you can find cases from a variety of states that construe the same type of ordinance, and offer these findings as persuasive evidence of how to interpret your own local ordinance.

Chapter 3

Researching Case Law

This chapter discusses the primary tools used to research case law. Part I discusses the tools used to find cases and to verify that the cases still are good law. It covers on-line research using Westlaw and Lexis and the primary print sources of digests, annotated law reports, and Shepard's Citations. Part II discusses case reporters and how to find the proper information from these sources for your research.

Part I – Case finders and verification sources

I.   FINDING CASES ON WESTLAW AND LEXIS

The simplest way to find cases in the modern legal world also is the most expensive: Westlaw and Lexis are far and away the most efficient sources with which to access case law—especially when used skillfully. With the exception of some truly old cases (those that are hundreds of years old, not just one hundred or one hundred fifty years old) and cases from other countries (which are beyond the scope of this book), Westlaw and Lexis are fast, efficient, and accurate in obtaining the case law that pertains to your issue. They are fee-based, so the benefits come at a great cost, but our discussion begins with these resources.

When you log on to Westlaw you will find a start screen that looks like this:

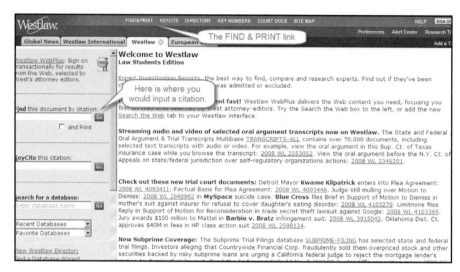

Alternatively, you can click on the FIND & PRINT link at the top of the page and pull up a new window that gives additional options for finding cases and other authorities:

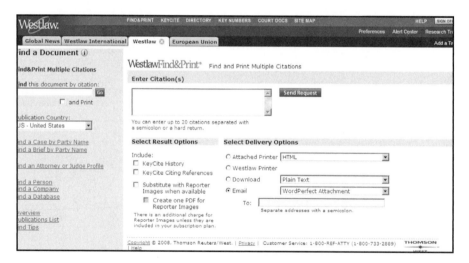

If you know the citation for a case, you simply can type in the volume number, reporter abbreviation, and page number in correct Bluebook or ALWD citation form or in some recognizable facsimile of the correct form. For instance, you could enter 433 F.3d 273 or 433 f.3d 273 or 433 f3d 273 or even 433f3d273 and in each case it would pull up United States v. Martha Stewart:

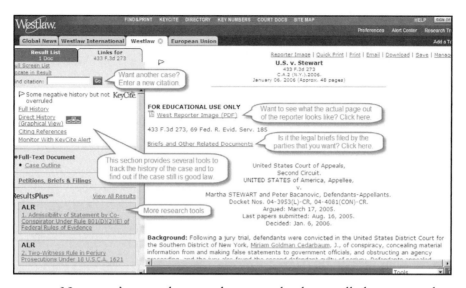

Now, you've got the case, but you also have called up a number of useful tools to assist you in the research process. On the left side of the image you can see a few of them. Westlaw has a built-in case history and verification service known as KeyCite that tracks historical information in the case. You can use this to find new cases that potentially are on the same point as the case you pulled up (the **Citing References** link shown above), and to verify that the case still is good law (the **Full History** and **Direct History** links shown above (See <u>section IV(A)(1) on Keycite</u> below). Westlaw surmises that if you are looking at <u>United States v. Martha Stewart</u>, you might be researching the evidence law issues of the case involving the admissibility of the statements of two co-conspirators, and so it offers you links to American Law Report annotations and other secondary sources (not captured in this image) on this and other points of law from the case.

You are not limited to looking at the electronically formatted version of the case; Westlaw provides a link to a .PDF version of the actual print form of the case as it appears in the reporter (if your Westlaw license allows access to this service). The PDF version is especially useful if you are printing the case for anyone that wants to see exactly how it appears in print, and the reporter's page numbers are a little easier to access in the PDF version (though you can also get this information from the Westlaw version if you know where to look).

You also might look up the briefs that the parties filed in the case before the court opinion was rendered; Westlaw provides a link to these documents, too. Though these briefs may prove enormously helpful in practice, you should make sure your legal writing professor or program permits consultation of such materials when you are working on a problem in a law school environment.

A.   Case law databases

When you are looking for more than one case for which you do not know the cite—for example, when you want to find *all* of the cases from a certain jurisdiction that are on the topic of your problem, you must first determine the set of files you want to search. Each on-line service provider maintains its case law in vast but well-organized databases. Westlaw calls them "Databases," while Lexis calls them "Sources." Databases are divided up by jurisdiction or topic or by level of court or by the relative age of the cases. The following are examples of different databases that can be searched on Westlaw:

WESTLAW DATABASE	SCOPE
ALLCASES	All state and federal cases. (<u>i.e.</u>, all levels of the state courts, U.S. Supreme Court, U.S. Courts of Appeals for all the circuits, all district courts)
ALLFEDS	All federal cases (U.S. Supreme Court, courts of appeals for all the circuits, all district courts) post 1945
-OLD <u>e.g.</u>, ALLFEDS-OLD	Added on to the end of certain databases, it retrieves older cases, usually pre-1945
SCT	U.S. Supreme Court cases post 1945
CTA	Court of Appeals cases from all circuits

CTAx	Court of Appeals cases from x Circuit (substitute the number of the circuit for the x; use DC for the D.C. Circuit)
<u>e.g.</u>, CTA2	Cases from the U.S. Court of Appeals for the Second Circuit
ALLSTATES	All state court cases from all published levels of the state courts
xx-CS	All state court cases from xx State (substitute the postal abbreviation for the state for the xx)
<u>e.g.</u>, MO-CS	All Missouri state court cases
xx-CS-ALL	All state and federal cases associated with xx State (xx is postal abbrev. for the state)
<u>e.g.</u>, IL-CS-ALL	All Illinois state cases, and federal cases from the U.S. Supreme Court, the Seventh Circuit and all district courts in Illinois
FEDx-ALL	Federal court cases from one circuit (x is the number of the circuit, or DC for D.C. circuit); U.S. Supreme Court, the circuit court identified, and all district courts within that circuit
<u>e.g.</u>, FED8-ALL	Federal court cases associated with the Eighth Circuit (U.S. Supreme Court, Eighth Circuit, and district courts in Missouri, Arkansas, Iowa, Minnesota,

North and South Dakota, and Nebraska

CTAx-ALL

All state and federal courts associated with (x) circuit

<u>e.g.</u> CTA8-ALL

Cases from the state and federal courts of the Eighth Circuit (U.S. Supreme Court, Eighth Circuit, and district court and state court cases from Missouri, Arkansas, Iowa, Minnesota, North and South Dakota and Nebraska

B.   Off-line time: planning your research

One obvious way to cut the cost of research on Westlaw and Lexis is to plan your research strategy ahead of time and formulate search queries before you go on-line and start running up the bill by punching in overbroad or random searches. Take some time before you log on to fig-

---

PRACTICE POINTER

Both Westlaw and Lexis have settings that enable you to search these services either by time spent on-line, or per each "transaction" (*e.g.*, each search you ask it to complete), and you should familiarize yourself with how to set and change these settings. If you plan to conduct numerous searches in a short span of time, perhaps because you need to cast a wide net to get your head around a legal issue before you can refine your research, you might elect to have the service charge you by time spent on-line. However, if you know enough to craft fewer, more limited, targeted searches, and you want to read through cases on-line, then transactional billing is the way to go.

---

ure out your search terms and even draft some initial search queries that you will run once you go on-line and log into the system. As we discuss in Chapter 8 of this volume, you should get in the habit of forming a **research plan** before you begin analyzing and researching the issues you've been asked to address.

As with statutory searching, the first thing to do is to break your problem down into key words, catch phrases, legal concepts, and terms of art that summarize the legal issues (legal questions) implicated by your problem. This process was explained in Chapter 2, but we repeat it here for your convenience.

The facts of the problem we addressed there were as follows: **A hunter with a rifle runs into someone's home in pursuit of a running deer and trips and falls and discharges his weapon injuring a housewife.**

From this, we derived several search terms:

Hunter, hunting, and negligence [party, action, potential claim for liability];

Weapons, guns, rifles and negligence with guns; weapons in household or indoors; accidental discharge of weapon; accidental shooting [actions and items involved in the problem];

Trespassing and negligence while trespassing; liability for damage or injury to property owner [potential liabilities to a party]

Unless you restrict your searches using the field restrictors discussed in Chapter 8, the searches you perform will search the full text of the documents in your chosen database for key words. Importantly, you have the ability to tell the on-line service to search for logical connections between words so that your results are more logical and relevant. Of course, you always want to draft a query that is more likely to bring up relevant, apposite authorities rather than inapposite, unhelpful authorities.

For example, you want to find dog-bite cases in Illinois. If you search and ask for every case in Illinois that has to do with dogs or bites, you'll get a plethora of cases—every civil and criminal case that has a canine actor or involving a dog in some way, and every case with a bite, whether from man or beast, and whether or not it was relevant to the cause of action—which typically means you will generate more cases than you need and many more than you can possibly review. But if you only search for dog within three words of bite (dog /3 bite), you will retrieve far fewer cases and ones that are much more likely to be useful to you.

We only scratched the surface of Boolean logic in Chapter 2, which you already may be familiar with from searching in library databases that you used as an undergraduate. Below we discuss the full power of what you can do with this system:

1.   Boolean logical connectors

When phrasing search queries, the same connectors will work in Westlaw and Lexis except as noted:

/x   Within x number of words, before or after.

      dog /3 bite   Will pull up any document where the word "dog" shows up three words ahead of or behind the word "bite."

In Lexis, you also can write this "w/x" – dog w/3 bite.

+x   Precedes by no more than x words.

      dog +2 bite   Will get you documents where "dog" precedes the word "bite" by no more than two words.

In Lexis, you can write this "pre/x" – dog pre/2 bite.

/s   Within the same sentence, before or after. A sentence is any string of words ending in a period, no matter how long or how many commas or semi-colons are in it. Each headnote in a West publication is one sentence.

      dog /s bite   Will pull up any document in which "dog" appears in the same sentence as "bite."

+s   Precedes in the same sentence.

       dog +s bite   Will get you documents where "dog" precedes the word "bite" in the same sentence.

/p   Within the same paragraph. A paragraph is any string of sentences divided by a hard return, no matter how long.

       dog /p bite   Pulls up any document in which "dog" appears in the same paragraph as "bite."

+p   Precedes in the same paragraph.

       dog +p bite   Will get you documents where "dog" precedes the word "bite" in the same paragraph. Not a very useful distinction.

&   Within the same document.

       dog & bite   Pulls up any document in which "dog" appears in the same document as "bite." Lots of cases.

Lexis makes you write out the word "and" – dog and bite.

%   But not in the same document as.

       dog % bite   Will pull up all cases with the word "dog" in them as long as the word "bite" is NOT also in the same document. If you want cases about dog breeds, dog shows, dog meat, or sales of dogs, and do not want to read any dog bite cases, you might use this.

RICO % Puerto	Gets you racketeering cases under the federal RICO statute without getting you every published case from Puerto Rico (But you will not get any RICO cases that are from Puerto Rico).

Lexis has an even nicer feature: not w/x. If you use this, you can specify cases with a certain word but not if it is within x words of another word.

dog not w/3 bite	In Lexis, this will get "dog" cases as long as the word appears further than three words from "bite" somewhere in the document, but "bite" can otherwise appear in the document. Less exclusive.

2.   Expanders and alternative forms

If you want to search for multiple words and synonyms as advised above, you need to express the concept of "or."

(a space)	In Westlaw, a space in your search query automatically means "or." dog canine w/3 bite biting chomp crunch scratch harm maul

Means:	dog or canine within three words of bite or biting or chomp or crunch or scratch or harm or maul

Lexis does not recognize spaces as "or" connectors. You must type the word "or" to express "or" – dog or canine w/3 bite or biting or chomp or crunch or scratch or harm or maul

* The asterisk is an expander that replaces a character in a word. This is useful if you are not sure of the spelling. It is also useful to use at the end of words to express multiple possible endings. You cannot use it at the beginning of a word. The number of * you chose limits the number of characters the service will add to your term: ** allows the service to add two characters; *** allows the service to add three.

wom*n	Will find both woman and women.
bath****	Will find bath, bathe, bathroom, bathing, bathmat, etc., but not bathtowel or bathhouse.
bank***	Will find bank, banks, banker, bankers, banking, etc., but not bankrupt, bankruptcy, etc.

NOTE: The asterisk is also useful to "trick" Westlaw into letting you search for words that Westlaw thinks are too common to be searched (it ordinarily will not let you proceed with a query that has such words in it such as "after" or "before" or "from"). You can work around this default logic by writing "af*er" "bef*re" and "fr*m," and Westlaw will let you search for these words.

! The exclamation point is a universal expander used at the end of a string of letters to allow searches for any possible endings.

bank!	Will find bank, banks, banker, bankers, banking, bankrupt, bankruptcy, bankroll, banknote, etc.

3.   Plurals and possessive forms

Normally, Westlaw and Lexis assume that you want the plurals and possessive forms of all the words you search, so they automatically pull up documents with the plurals and possessives in them. "**Dog**" will get you dogs and dog's and dogs' and "**plaintiff**" will get you plaintiffs, plaintiff's, and plaintiffs'. Unusual plurals (women, mice, geese, indices, memoranda, etc.) are ***not*** picked up, so search for them in addition to your singular terms. The same goes for unusual singulars (datum, criterion, alumnus, etc.), and possessives (my, mine, his). If you ***only*** want the singular or the plural of a word, you could try using but not (%) to exclude the form you do not want. *e.g.*, procedure % procedures. You potentially would exclude a lot of documents that you really do want. In Lexis, you have to take different unusual measures that your trainer can fill you in on.

4.   Acronyms, abbreviations, and compound words

Search for single-letter abbreviated words and acronyms in this way:

R.I.C.O.	Will get you RICO, R I C O, R. I. C. O., and R.I.C.O.
F.R.C.P.	Will get you FRCP, F R C P, F. R. C. P., and F.R.C.P.

Search for potentially compounded words with a hyphen in between:

whistle-blower	Will get you: whistleblower, whistle blower, and whistle-blower.
dog-catcher	Will get you: dogcatcher, dog catcher, and dog-catcher.

5.   Phrases

In Westlaw, you should put any specific phrases that you want to match in quotes – Westlaw will pull up both exact matches and some nearly exact matches:

"beyond a reasonable doubt"   Will also get you "beyond reasonable doubt" or "beyond the reasonable doubt."

You can still use an expander if you are not sure of the spelling or if you think multiple endings are possible:

"res ipsa loquit*r"   Will get you "res ipsa loquitor" and "res ipsa loquitur."

"wheels of justice grind exceedingly fine!"   Will find the phrase no matter if it ends in "fine" or "finely" in various documents.

In Lexis, the system does not think of spaces as "or" connectors, so you do not need quotation marks for phrases:

res ipsa loquit*r   Still gets you "res ipsa loquitor" and "res ipsa loquitur."

6.   Putting it all together—use expanders and connectors to make a better search

Using the connectors and the expanders allows you to construct a search for synonyms and varying forms. Our initial search terms could be combined in many different ways that take advantage of synonyms and alternative phrasing for the concepts listed here. One example, using the Boolean logical relationship of "within the same sentence" (in Westlaw, /s) to connect groups of terms, and leaving a space between individual terms to connote the "or" concept, would be:

> hunter hunting /s weapon rifle gun /s accident accidental negligent negligence injure injuring trespass trespassing trespasser

This could be shortened using the universal ending function (in Westlaw, **!**). For example, using this ending on "hunt" would mean that "**hunt!**" as a search term will retrieve: hunt hunts hunter hunting and any other word with the first four letters "hunt." We would then modify our search as follows:

> **hunt! /s weapon rifle gun /s accident! negligen! injur! trespass!**

7.   Revise and re-search again and again

If you get too few results (or none), add synonyms and alternate terms and loosen the space of connections between words (e.g., move from within five words, /5, to within a sentence, /s, or from /s to within a paragraph, /p, or within the same document, &):

> **hunt! stalk! chas*** sport /p weapon gun rifle pistol bullet /p home house household indoors /p shoot! shot accident! discharge "went off" fir*** kill*** & neglig! liab! culpab!**

If you get too many (50+) cases the first time you run the search, revise your search, tighten up the connectors, drop some of the expanders, or leave out some of the alternative terms you first used:

> **hunt! chas*** /8 weapon gun rifle /s home house household indoors /10 shoot! shot accident! discharge "went off" fir*** kill*** /p neglig! liab! culpab!**

Try this again and again until you get a reasonable number of documents to look at.

C.   Interpreting search results

Now that we have our searches worked out, we can go on-line and run them. The choice of database on Westlaw is based on the law applicable to the problem. There are many federal database permutations (refer back to section I(A) above), but figuring out the identifier for a state case law database is as simple as putting the suffix –CS behind the state's postal abbreviation. We will find Louisiana state cases in the LA-CS database:

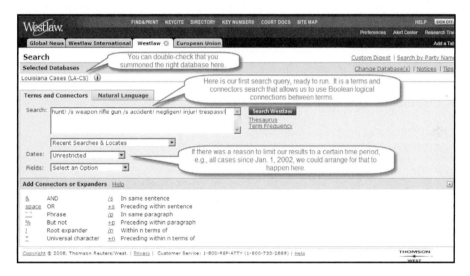

Running this search produces the following results page:

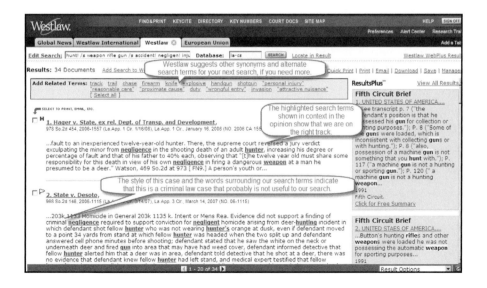

As you can see, the most prominent part of this page is the list of search results, shown with your search terms highlighted and in the context of the opinion where the terms appear. This is just a partial screen capture of a much longer list. And note that the search results are not the only thing presented here, because Westlaw offers other search tools: alternate terms and synonyms for your search terms that you might want to add to a future search, and additional research tools (starting with the appellate briefs shown on the right side of this screen capture). If we scroll down we will see more tools displayed, including annotated law reports (ALR) and secondary sources including encyclopedias and treatises (American Jurisprudence and American Law of Products Liability):

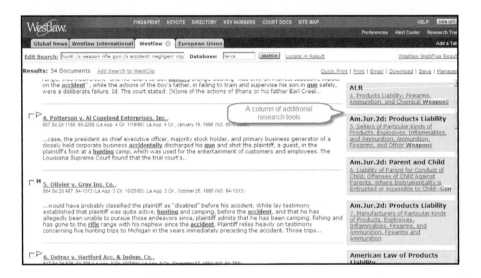

The advantage to this approach is the one-stop shopping aspect of the service, which includes reminders to check additional sources in the course of your research. While most researchers learn to ignore a lot of these suggested sources and cross-selling techniques by the service, in your early years these suggestions can be quite useful in helping you flesh out your research and in reminding you to consult case finders and secondary sources rather than simply relying on case law database searches for your research.

The eighth item on the results list (not shown in the screen captures above) looks like it is most clearly on point, and because it is from the Louisiana Supreme Court, it provides a good starting point in using the search results to pursue your research. When you click on the link for the eighth item, you will pull up a case report screen:

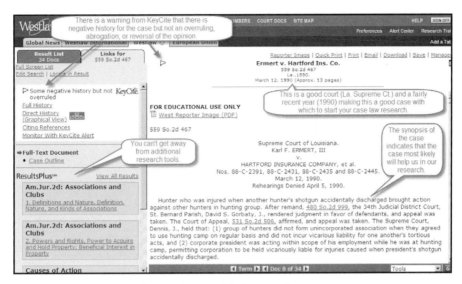

West, like many other publishers of cases, prints a synopsis or summary of the opinion as the first paragraph under the style or caption of the case. This paragraph is not part of the actual opinion and has no precedential value (the actual opinion begins with the judge's name or other author designation such as Per Curiam), but it often is a useful starting point to see if a case that contains your search terms is actually on point. The synopsis above should give you hope that this case is in fact on point on our research problem with the hunter.

Perhaps the greatest strength of the on-line fee-based services is in the contents of the opinion, where statutes and case law cited and relied on by the court is hyper-linked, and in the Full History and Citing References section (in the KeyCite sidebar), where later cases and secondary sources citing the case at hand also are hyper-linked. These two features are revealed in the images below:

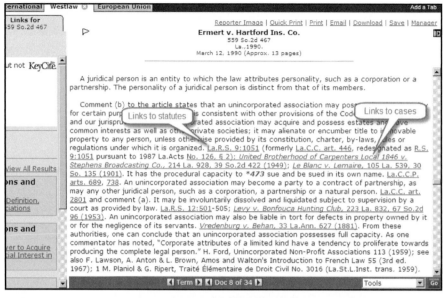

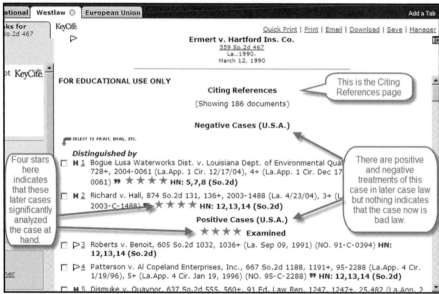

By using the tools displayed on these pages, you can use one solidly on-point case to find other on-point cases. Some of the later cases may be critical of the first case and others will support it or follow it or move the law in new directions. All of this is beneficial to your research on the issue.

The Citing References page on Westlaw assigns a one to four star rating based on the level of discussion of the case at hand in subsequent cases. Four stars is the highest rating indicating a significant level of discussion, and the ratings go down from there. Westlaw explains the ratings in this way:

★ ★ ★ ★ ("Examines")   means the citing authority really talks a great deal about the case, often in a page or more of the citing authority

★ ★ ★ ("Discusses")   means the citing authority cites and discusses the case, usually in more than a paragraph but less than a full page

★ ★ ("Cites")   means the citing authority cites the case but only has a short discussion, usually in less than a full paragraph or footnote

★ ("Mentioned")   means the citing authority only cites it in passing, usually in a string cite, with no significant discussion of the case.

Flagging symbols are used by each on-line service to warn you of developments in the subsequent history of an authority. Westlaw uses little flags, Lexis uses little highway road signs.

⚑ Red Flag; ⬤ Stop Sign   The case is bad law, meaning it has been reversed, overturned, abrogated, or severely criticized by a proper authority on at least one legal issue. (You should check to see which issue was overturned, because even a red flagged case is appropriate to rely on for issues that have not been overruled.)

▷ Yellow Flag; ⚠ Caution Sign

> The case has some negative history, usually criticism from a later court, but the on-line service still thinks it is good law.

PRACTICE POINTER

Flags that cry wolf?
We have found some tendency on the part of the on-line services to "overuse" the yellow flag, so don't be too quick to avoid using cases that have such warnings attached. Many leading U.S. Supreme Court cases come with yellow flags. For example, see *Lawrence v. Texas*, 539 U.S. 558. Although *Lawrence* still is squarely good law, *Lawrence* generates yellow flags because lower courts have declined to extend it to different factual circumstances. That certainly does not mean you should not cite *Lawrence* (but the flags should serve as a reminder to investigate how your jurisdiction has interpreted and applied the decision). And while we are on the topic: even red flags should be investigated before you reject a case outright, because sometimes only one issue not at all relevant to your problem has been rendered bad law.

Other symbols are used to show non-detrimental subsequent history:

H Blue H (Westlaw); ◆ Green + (Lexis)

> The case has subsequent history, such as a later opinion in the same case, or the opinion was affirmed, or certiorari was denied, or some other neutral or positive history has occurred.

C Green C (Westlaw); Ⓐ Blue A (Lexis)

> The case has been cited neutrally or favorably by other authorities.

Westlaw also has coded the on-line opinions it reports in accordance with the headnotes it prints in its national reporting system and the Key Number system used throughout its digest system, both of which are described in the next section.

By placing all of these resources just a mouse-click away, Westlaw and Lexis give you a rewarding research experience for your dollar, but those dollars can rack up quickly. That statement alone should reveal to you the ever-present need to consider other sources for researching cases in addition to these fee-based services. There will be times when your superiors will not permit you to use the fee-based services, or your clients decide that they cannot or will not afford the cost of these services. The good news is that even in these situations, there are perfectly acceptable substitutes, including the print resources discussed in the section below, that initially may strike you as more time-consuming to use but will allow you to exhaust the field for acquiring cases on your issue.

PRACTICE POINTER

Especially in specialized areas of law, you may find enormously helpful print-based resources—mini-treatises or practice guides—that you will want to keep at your fingertips for beginning any research project and likely will become your first stop for getting your head around a new issue. In addition, and even though many print resources are also available electronically, you should keep in mind that print resources can force you to think about a legal problem in a way that electronic searching cannot duplicate or replace. That's because when you pick up a print volume—of a digest, for example—you may see things (synonyms, other potential causes of action) for which you were not looking but which may be enormously useful to you as you think through your research problem. You thus (quite literally) may be able to enlarge your line of vision about how to approach a case by looking at how the information in a print volume is organized, by seeing what information surrounds and cross-references the terms you think may be relevant.

II.   FINDING CASES USING DIGESTS

A.   A digest and its indices

When you are given a legal problem and you set off to use a digest to find cases that discuss this legal problem, once again, the first thing to do is to break your problem down into catch words, legal concepts, or brief phrases that summarize the legal issues implicated by your problem. The gateway to the digests is their indices, and the indices are organized into alphabetical lists of key words, brief phrases, and legal concepts.

hunter hunting

weapon rifle gun

accident accidental negligent negligence injure injuring

trespass trespassing trespasser

Digests themselves are organized by catch words (key words), concepts, and short phrases. They present cases dealing with those catch words, concepts and phrases. The index to the digests, often called a "descriptive word index," lists and cross-references these and other related key words, concepts and short phrases. Even if you do not come up with the exact key word from your problem, you often will find a cross-reference that leads you to the correct term. *E.g.*, "gun" will cross-reference you to "weapons;" "dog" will cross-reference you to "animals;" "hunting" will cross-reference you to "negligence–sports and recreation."

Another nice thing about digests is that they are organized by region (national, regional, or state) or jurisdiction (federal vs. state) or subject matter (bankruptcy, military law) so that you can more readily zero in on the best cases for your problem.

If you cannot find cases using the most promising words and concepts, broaden your inquiry into these other areas. Read all the "Hunting" headnotes. Read further in the "Weapons, Guns" headnotes. Think of synonyms for your initial words and concepts and search for them.

Here is an illustration of the process using West's Michigan Digest 2d:

First, look up WEAPONS in the Descriptive Word Index

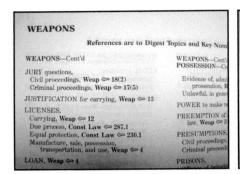

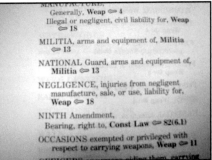

Then find the WEAPONS section in the correct volume of the digest.

Note the beginning page for the topic of WEAPONS below. It lists the subjects covered and subjects ***not*** covered in the West topic of WEAPONS, so that you can figure out quickly if WEAPONS is a digest topic that you want to research.

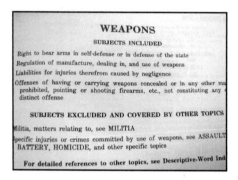

Within the topic of WEAPONS, the index told us to look at sub-topic (Key Number) 18 on negligence:

Here, you can find the Michigan cases on the sub-topic of negligence in the use of weapons (including and, for some reason, starting with federal cases applying Michigan law on this topic).

Don't forget to check out the **pocket part** in the back of the digest to find the most recent cases.

B.   West's digests and the key number system

West is the King of Digests, just as it is the King of Case Law. Common features of West digests are:

1.   Legal situations are divided into seven major categories:

Persons

Property

Contracts

Torts

Crimes

Remedies

Government

2.   Categories are subdivided into more than 415 topics which are arranged in one alphabetical sequence and are numbered.

Example:

92. Constitutional Law

DIGEST TOPICS

See, also, Outline of the Law by Seven Main Divisions of Law, preceding this section

The topic numbers shown below may be used in WESTLAW searches for cases within the topic and within specified key numbers.

1	Abandoned and Lost Property	42	Assumpsit, Action of	79	Clerks of Courts
		43	Asylums	80	Clubs
2	Abatement and Revival	44	Attachment	81	Colleges and Universities
4	Abortion and Birth Control	45	Attorney and Client		
		46	Attorney General	82	Collision
5	Absentees	47	Auctions and Auctioneers	83	Commerce
6	Abstracts of Title			83H	Commodity Futures Trading Regulation
7	Accession	48	Audita Querela		
8	Accord and Satisfaction	48A	Automobiles	84	Common Lands
		48B	Aviation	85	Common Law
9	Account	49	Bail	88	Compounding Offenses
10	Account, Action on	50	Bailment		
11	Account Stated	51	Bankruptcy	89	Compromise and Settlement
11A	Accountants	52	Banks and Banking		
12	Acknowledgement	54	Beneficial Associations	89A	Condominium
13	Action			90	Confusion of Goods
14	Action on the Case	55	Bigamy	91	Conspiracy
15	Adjoining Landowners	56	Bills and Notes	92	Constitutional Law
		58	Bonds	92B	Consumer Credit
15A	Administrative Law and Procedure	59	Boundaries	92H	Consumer Protection
		60	Bounties		
16	Admiralty	61	Breach of Marriage Promise	93	Contempt
17	Adoption			95	Contracts
18	Adulteration	62	Breach of the Peace	96	Contribution
19	Adultery	63	Bribery	97	Conversion
20	Adverse Possession	64	Bridges	98	Convicts
21	Affidavits	65	Brokers	99	Copyrights and Intellectual Property
23	Agriculture	66	Building and Loan Associations		

Each topic is subdivided into specific sub-topics—words, concepts, phrases, and assigned a **key number**. This is written as the topic followed by the Key symbol ⌐ followed by the key number.

Example:

Constitutional Law ⌐ 89 Liberty to contract

Constitutional Law ⌐ 90 Freedom of speech and of the press

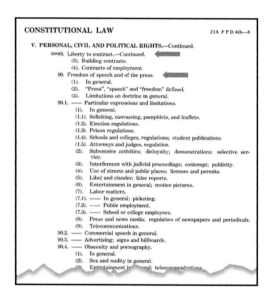

On Westlaw, the topic name (e.g., Constitutional Law) is replaced by its number (92) and the key symbol ⌐ is replaced by the letter "k". Example: 92k89 =Constitutional Law, Liberty to contract; 92k90 = Constitutional Law, Freedom of speech and of the press:

These key numbers correspond to the same sub-topic (word, concept, phrase, issue) *in every digest published by West.* The sub-topics in turn correspond to the headnotes you find at the beginning of every case published by West. If you find a good headnote in a case, you can get the key number off that headnote and go to any West digest and look up other potentially relevant cases that contain that same sub-topic identified by the key number.

C.   How do you find what topics and key numbers to look up?

Common features of West's Key Number System used to find topics and key numbers and thereafter to find relevant cases include:

Descriptive Word Index	When you look up a word or short phrase from your list of issues, this index will show you sub-topics and key numbers associated with your word or short phrase.

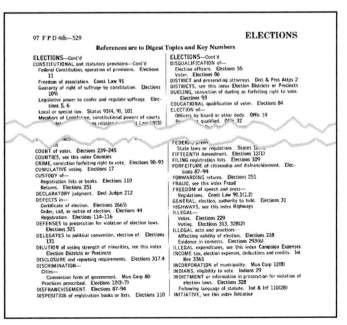

Topic Outlines, Analysis

Each topical section of the digest (e.g., Contracts; Weapons; Racketeer Influenced and Corrupt Organizations) begins with a listing of the subjects covered by that topic and the subjects that are excluded and handled elsewhere. Therefore, you will know if you are looking in the right topical section.

Following that is a detailed outline of the sub-topics and key numbers covered under the general topic at hand.

Table of Cases

If you know the name of a case on point, you can look it up here and find the key numbers associated with that case; then you can look up these key numbers in the digest to find other cases on point. (Previously, these tables were organized using the plaintiff's name only, but more recently, digests have created parallel entries for each case which are arranged according to the defendant's name; e.g., "Wade, Roe v." will be listed in addition to "Roe v. Wade.")

Defendant-Plaintiff Table	Some digest volumes still have these. They were used to find the full name of a case on point where you only knew the defendant's name. More recently, these volumes have been rendered obsolete because digest tables of cases have started creating parallel entries for each case which are arranged according to the defendant's name, as described in the entry above.
Words and Phrases	Special volume presenting words and phrases from cases (*i.e.*, words and phrases that are judicially defined), and listing a case or two that have these words or phrases in them. From there, you look up the cases in a Table of Cases, or find the case itself, and from there find out the headnotes associated with the case. Note: not every digest series has these volumes. The American Digest Series (Decennial Digests, General Digests) and the Regional Digests don't have them.
Popular Name Tables	Within a digest or by themselves, these tables point you to the correct name of cases that have developed a more popular name, such as the "Right to Die" case (<u>Cruzan v. Director, Missouri Dep't of Health</u>), or the "Abortion Rights" case (<u>Roe v. Wade</u>). Again, not every digest series prints these.

Key Number	If you already know a key number, you can look up other cases having head notes with that same key number.
Advance Pamphlet and Pocket Parts	Don't forget to look for the most recent cases in the digest's advance pamphlet volumes and pocket parts.
Advance Sheets	The advance sheets for each West reporter have a mini-digest covering the headnote abstracts for the cases reported in the advance sheets. They come out as frequently as weekly.

D.   West's Digest Series

1.   West's United States Supreme Court Digest

Provides access to U.S. Supreme Court decisions back to 1790. Listings are by subject and case name.

2.   Federal Practice Digest

A series of five successive series of digests which cover decisions of the federal court system. U.S. Supreme Court cases are listed first, then the U.S. Court of Appeals cases by order of circuit, then the U.S. District Court cases are listed alphabetically by state and district within the state (*e.g.*, California district court cases are listed before Colorado district court cases, and Northern District of California cases before Southern District of California cases). The series runs as follows:

Federal Digest, cases through 1938

Modern Federal Practice, 1939-1960

Federal Practice Digest 2d, 1961-Nov. 1975

Federal Practice Digest 3d, Dec. 1975-1983[1]

Federal Practice Digest 4th, 1984 forward[1]

3.   Regional digests

West publishes seven regional reporters but only four regional digests: Atlantic, Southern, Northwestern, and Pacific Digests. Regional digests include cases for each of the states in the region. Headnotes under a key number are arranged alphabetically by state.

4.   State digests

West publishes a state digest for 47 states. They have more comprehensive coverage than regional digests—they include the cases from the state's courts and cases from federal courts that arise from the state or involve the law of the state (*e.g.*, The Florida Digest includes U.S. Supreme Court and U.S. Court of Appeals, Eleventh Circuit cases that arise from Florida or involve Florida law).

5.   American Digest System

Modestly described as the "Master Index to all the Case Law of our Country," this is West's attempt to beat the world to digest all recent opinions. There are three components—Century Edition, Decennial Digests, and General Digests.

---

1   There was some unusual compilation of headnotes of cases from Dec. 1975 to Dec. 1983—some were categorized in the Fed. Prac. Digest 3d and some in the Fed. Prac. Digest 4th, so to locate cases from this period you should refer to both the 3d and the 4th series of the Fed. Prac. Digest.

a.   Century Edition Digest 1658-1896

Since the National Reporter System did not exist during this period, there were no key numbers. Volumes 21-25 of the 1st Decennial Digest has a Table of Cases from this period and an index can be found at the end of vol. 50 of the Century Edition Digest.

b.   Decennial Digests 1897-2001

Issued every ten years. (Since 1981, they are issued in two parts every five years). Each series contains a Table of Cases, Descriptive Word Index, List of Subjects included and excluded at the start of each topical section. The 2nd and 3rd Decennial key numbers are cross-referenced to section numbers in the Century Digest.

c.   General Digests 2001-Present (in progress)

Because Decennial Digests are not supplemented or updated, General Digest volumes contain the latest headnotes in all West Reporters. They are arranged by topic; each volume has a table of key numbers covered in the volume. You will not find things fast enough looking volume by volume, however, so a cumulative table of topics covered in the preceding ten volumes is included in each 10th volume.

6.   Specialized digests

West publishes five specialized digests: Bankruptcy Digest, Military Justice Digest, U.S. Federal Claims Digest, Education Law Digest, U.S. Merit Systems Protection Board Digest. As suggested by the titles, these digests are focused on particular kinds of cases.

E.   Other digests

Looseleaf services and private reporting services (BNA, CCH) sometimes have digests to accompany their looseleaf publications. American Law Reports has its own digest series.

III. FINDING CASES USING ANNOTATED LAW REPORTS

A. Annotations and Annotated Law Reports

Annotations are articles that collect cases on a single legal topic. Arguably, they are prompted by a new and interesting case—perhaps even a watershed case with groundbreaking effect—in a certain area of the law. The case is reprinted in the reports along with annotations and commentary that summarize, collect cases, and provide the background and legal context for the case and the specific area of the law involved in the case. Hence the name, "annotation."

Annotations are often drafted to address a point of legal ambiguity or controversy (at least one that arguably exists at the time of their publication). An editor will take on an issue which, due to a court decision, legislation, or some other "legal event," has become unsettled, or when one that was unsettled becomes settled.

Annotations are somewhat similar to a case comment in a law review, but generally they are written more objectively (less argumentatively). The purpose of the annotated law report is not to assert a point of view or propose a solution to a legal conundrum but to collect cases and present a useful outline and summary of the law on a certain, specific topic. Thus, they can be more useful to the practitioner who may not want to wade through someone's thesis and argument in a law review article.

Annotations are very specific. You will not always find one on the topic you want, but when you do, it can be like striking research gold. An annotation on a related topic may be of some use to you, but the best annotations are those that hit your issue on all fours.

B. Using Annotations

Annotations are another way to find and collect cases on your topic of interest. They are also a secondary source of the law, but only middling in terms of persuasiveness. Like a treatise, hornbook, or legal encyclopedia, they can provide you with a basic grounding in a specific area of the law so that you can understand a problem that your client has brought to you or your law office. Again, they are so specific that at times you cannot always find one that serves your particular need. But when you do, they can really give a great deal of relevant law that is directly on point.

C.   Who Writes Them

Editors at the publishing company or freelance editors write annotations. One author per annotation is the norm. The author is a lawyer, but you probably will not know who she is or how good a lawyer she is. Therefore, don't bet the client's farm on what you find in an annotation. That said, they can be extremely useful for forging a path into researching an area of law that you know little about.

Use a great deal of caution when you are thinking of citing an annotation. They are a secondary source of law and carry some weight with the judges and lawyers who like them, but they are middling in persuasiveness at best. Also be aware that not everyone likes them or uses them, and you probably will not know a particular judge's likes and dislikes ahead of time.

D.   American Law Reports—the Granddaddy of Them All

American Law Reports (A.L.R.) are synonymous in some peoples' minds with annotated law reports, and this generalization is not that far from the truth. A.L.R. dominates the field of annotated law reports. That the abbreviation is the same for both is no accident.

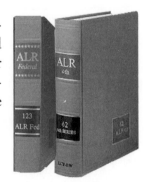

1.   Function of A.L.R.s

Some lawyers use A.L.R.s as a primary case-finding resource in place of digests. Others use them as a tertiary resource, a last ditch effort to find cases that they cannot find anywhere else. Probably neither practice is the best way to make use of them. A.L.R.s are

more than merely a "case finding index," although this is one of their functions. Annotation editors try to collect all of the relevant judicial opinions,
statutory and regulatory law—in theory,
all the relevant law—then analyze and
organize it into a useful commentary.
The editors look to all jurisdictions, state
and federal, wherever relevant law may
be found, and attempt to present it to
the researcher in a logical, coherent fashion. Thus, A.L.R.s should be viewed and
optimally used as a *complement* to digests
and other case-finding resources.

2. Researching
Cases with A.L.R.s

A.L.R.s are found on Westlaw in the ALR database. They also are
cross-referenced automatically as a research tool when you run searches in

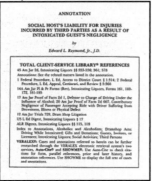

Westlaw's databases.

In print form, the key to the A.L.R.s is their indices. You can

locate A.L.R.s with the A.L.R. Index, periodically republished (and check for pocket parts), and with intervening "Quick Index" supplements that fill in between republications of the general index:

From there, you can find the annotations, if any, on your topic:

Each A.L.R. has an Outline and Index, a Table of Jurisdictions whose cases are cited in the annotation, and the actual text of the annotation:

3.   Limitations of A.L.R.s

Do not be seduced by the attractiveness of the A.L.R. package. There are certain things that A.L.R.s do well, but there are several things they do **not** do:

- They do not "answer" the legal question, but organize relevant authority around and about that issue so that the researcher can efficiently investigate, analyze and eventually draft the writing that answers the question at hand.

- They are not jurisdiction specific, so you will have to sort through a lot of information to find relevant and controlling authorities from your jurisdiction, and you will probably have to do follow-up research based on the controlling and persuasive authorities you do find. (This is probably their single, most important draw-back.)

- They are not written like a proper office memorandum. They have an outline, but it is not the kind of outline that you should use to draft a proper office memorandum. Some uninformed individuals might consider an A.L.R. annotation to be a good "paper." Not so. Besides constituting plagiarism, that belief misapprehends the annotations' purpose, which is to assemble the relevant law so that the researcher can get quickly to important and relevant information—the issues and cases that define the client's problem. They will not give you or your client an answer, just resources toward the answer.

- A.L.R.s are focused on narrow, specific legal issues, particularly those that are troublesome and unsettled, rather than on general catch words, phrases and key number concepts like West's digests are. It is often hit or miss with A.L.R.s, whereas digests will almost always find you something relevant to work with.

4.   A.L.R. series

First series of A.L.R.—1919 to 1948

Second series (A.L.R. 2d)—1948 to 1965

Third series (A.L.R. 3d)—1965 to 1980

Fourth series (A.L.R. 4th) —1980 to 1992

Fifth series (A.L.R. 5th)—1992 to present (ongoing).

A.L.R. Federal (A.L.R. Fed.)—1969 to present (ongoing). Limited to federal questions. As a result, federal issues are not covered in the last part of the A.L.R. 3d and 4th and 5th.

5.   Updating older A.L.R.s

As you can see, the A.L.R. series has been going on for quite some time, and many of the annotations you will find in your research will be crusty with age. Fortunately, A.L.R.s have several updating resources:

- A.L.R. 3rd, 4th, and 5th and A.L.R. Fed. are updated by pocket parts.

- A.L.R. 2d are updated by a separate hard-bound publication, called the "Later Case Service," which usually is shelved with the A.L.R. 2d. Then someone realized that a hard-bound volume would itself quickly go out of date. Whoops! So, the Later Case Service got its own pocket parts.

• Don't worry about the first series of A.L.R.—they are too old to fuss over. For the antiquarian in the group, the series is updated with paperback books which are not published for each volume and are not cumulative—in other words, you have fish through all of them. Then there are something referred to as Blue Book of Supplemental Decisions, in seven volumes.

6.   Verifying the accuracy of A.L.R.s

Aside from the usual "shelf-life" problems addressed above, sometimes the law in a particular area changes drastically and rapidly. An annotation can go bad if it is not refrigerated. The freon for this refrigeration is the "Annotation History Table," which is found in the very back of the Annotations' General Index (currently in six volumes, usually shelved at the end of all the A.L.R.s). The history table tells you if an entirely new annotation was written to replace or "supersede" an earlier one. It will also tell you if a second annotation was written to amend or "supplement" an earlier one.

The Annotation History Table is organized by its respective A.L.R. series, then by customary citation form for each annotation. If your annotation is not listed, then it has not been superseded or supplemented (but check the **index's** own pocket part to be sure!). If it is listed, there will be a reference to the supplementing or superseding A.L.R. annotation.

IV.   RESOURCES TO VERIFY YOUR RESEARCH SOURCES

A.   On-line verification resources: Westlaw's KeyCite and Lexis's Shepard's Citations

If your sources are bad law, they are of no value to you whatsoever, and if you rely on them to render legal advice or to argue a point on behalf of your client, you are committing malpractice. Therefore, you absolutely must use a verification resource to check the status of your research results. The efficient and convenient (and yes, arguably the most expensive) ones to use are the on-line verification service offered by Westlaw---KeyCite---and that offered by Lexis---Shepard's on-line service. We say "arguably" the most expensive, however, because the technology of the on-line services has advanced to such a degree that it is far more time-consuming (and if you are billing time, that's money, too) to handle updating and verifying your research results in any other way. Accordingly, even places of business (and clients) that do not permit researching with fee-based services will permit you to use KeyCite or Shepard's online to check the status of the research results you produce.

1.   KeyCite

KeyCite is accessible from any Westlaw screen by clicking on the KeyCite tab. From there you pull up a KeyCite start screen where you can input a citation:

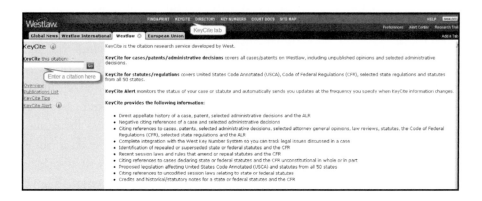

You also can run KeyCite to check an authority while you are looking at it on Westlaw by clicking one of the KeyCite links in the left column to pull up a case history or a table of citing references:

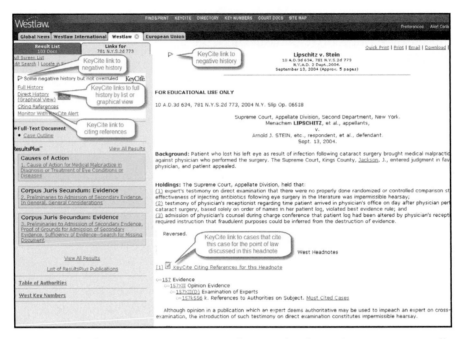

Whichever access point you choose, the direct history report tells the tale of what has happened to the case on direct review and reports any direct or indirect attacks on the precedential value of the case.

What is an *indirect* attack? If a subsequent case has cited the case you are viewing, it will be listed in KeyCite. If the case treated the opinion in a certain way (criticized, followed, explained, distinguished, limited, and others) or your case was cited in a dissent from the listed case, this will be coded in the list. Therefore, if a case expressly overturns, abrogates, or criticizes your case (by name), it will show up in KeyCite even though the attack did not come on direct review of an appeal or writ petition. Westlaw also claims that if a later case attacks a group of cases that all have the same holding or rely on common authority, or if one case in the line of subsequent history gets negative treatment, KeyCite will even pick up on this kind of indirect attack even if the authority you are checking is not actually cited in the later case.

You can review the direct history in list form:

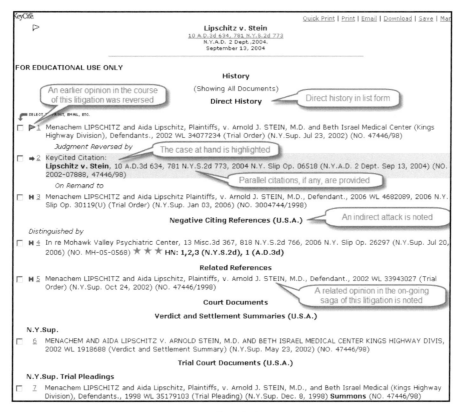

Or you can see it in a graphical depiction:

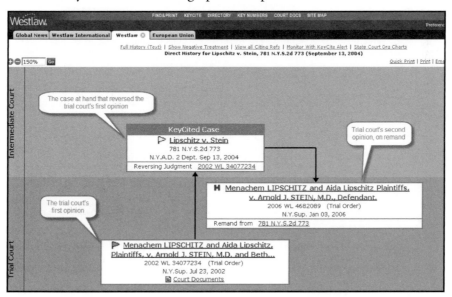

In either case, KeyCite gives you the parallel citations, if any, for the case at hand and other cases in the direct history of the case.

The **citing references** report tells the tale of the later cases and other authorities (mainly secondary authorities) that have cited the case. As discussed above, there are codes for the level of treatment (★ o n e star to ★ ★ ★ ★ four stars) and whether the citing reference quotes the case (shown by a 99 symbol). If the citing authority discusses points of law found in the headnotes of the case, these also are identified:

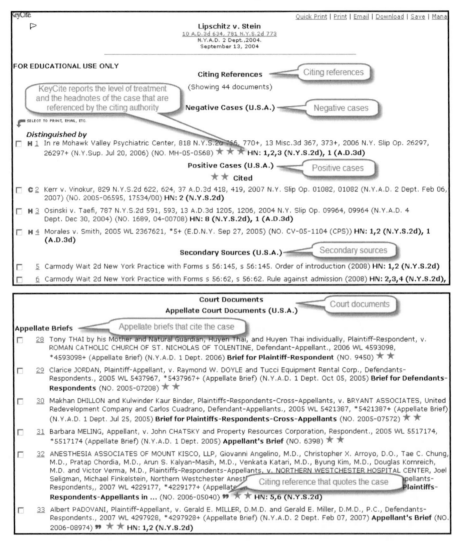

KeyCite is not just for cases. You can check the viability of statutes and administrative law in KeyCite to see if the statutory section is subject to new or proposed legislation or has been amended or repealed or otherwise invalidated, and you can check to see if an administrative law provision is subject to amendment or proposed rule-making.

2.   Shepard's Citations on-line

Shepard's is very similar to KeyCite. It might rankle the Shepard's people to hear us say that, because Shepard's was *the original, one and only* case-verification service in the print-media-only days (see section B below). Hard to imagine now given how cumbersome it was to use them. Shepard's On-Line is a stand-alone service but it also may be accessed through Lexis, as shown below:

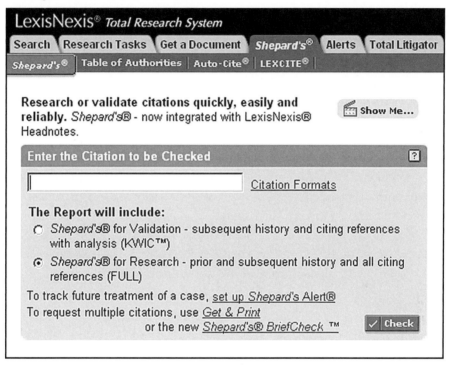

Shepard's On-Line provides direct history (the Summary shown above) and citing references (called Citing Decisions), and provides the parallel citations, if any, to the original case and the citing decisions. As with KeyCite, references to the point of law in headnotes are tracked, in this case the headnotes from the LexisNexis version of the case are tracked rather than the headnotes from the West publication of the case.

3.   Updating KeyCite or Shepards?

Do you need to update your on-line KeyCite or Shepard's information? **No!** The great thing about KeyCite and Shepard's on-line is that the reports you pull up when you check a citation are cumulative and comprehensive; you do not have to run the same cite through multiple databases in the same way that you have to pull multiple volumes of the print version of Shepard's off the shelves in order to check one citation. Thus, using the on-line version of these cite checking services, although fee based, may actually save your client money. What you pay for the on-line service may well be offset by the time saved in not having to pull and pour over multiple volumes in order to check each cite (and time is money). Of course, if your research lingers over the course of several weeks, or if you are in the middle of a lawsuit or other long-running legal project, you should recheck your authorities periodically to see if something new has developed in their history or citing references.

4.   Finding other cases using "One Good Case" with KeyCite or Shepard's

KeyCite and Shepard's also are an effective tool for finding other relevant cases (and A.L.R. annotations, and secondary sources such as treatises and law review articles)—namely those that cite the good cases you have already found and are KeyCiting or Shepardizing. And of course the same can be said for the bad cases you found—don't ignore them. KeyCite or Shepardize them to find the citing references for other bad cases that you need to distinguish and handle. This works even if you only have one good headnote from a case—KeyCite and Shepard's will list and code the particular cases that have cited your case for the proposition stated in each of the headnotes found in your case.

B.   Print resources: Shepard's Citations in print form

In 1873, Frank Shepard said, "We all worry about whether these cases we are relying on are getting overturned, criticized, followed, or just ignored and abandoned; someone should keep track of this." Someone (Frank's wife?) said, "Frank - put your money where your mouth is. You keep track of them! If you do a good job, they'll name a verb after you."

And he did. Frank set about to compile volumes that list all the cases that cite other cases, and he encoded the list to show if the citing case did damage to the original case. He did such a bang-up job that, just as his wife predicted, we use the verb "to Shepardize" to refer to process of verifying our cases in honor of old Frank.

For verification resources in *print media*, there is no substitute for Shepard's Citations. For a hundred thirty-five years, the only print resource to accurately and exhaustively verify that cases still are good law has been Shepard's. Nevertheless, one of the most startling changes in legal research in the last ten years has been law school and law firm libraries' near total abandonment of print Shepard's volumes. With budgets perennially pinched, and the cost of print volumes of every kind rising each year, most libraries have cut back on their subscriptions to Shepard's in print form, and many libraries have abandoned carrying the volumes altogether. If you find Shepard's books in a law library at all these days, the library likely is only subscribing to the volumes covering state cases of the state in which the library is located. It is a tribute to the effectiveness of the on-line versions of Shepard's and its competitor, KeyCite, that libraries have stopped buying Shepard's in print form.

1.   The codes used in Shepard's

For those of you limited to the print volumes or simply interested in a bit of citatory history, Shepard's uses the following codes to explain how a listed case affects the case you are Shepardizing:

a	affirmed (<u>i.e.</u>, the listed case affirms the case you are Shepardizing)
c	criticized
d	distinguished
e	explained
f	followed
h	harmonized (the listed case differs from your case, but reconciles the differences between itself and your case)
j	dissenting opinion (a dissenting opinion cites the case you are Shepardizing)
L	limited (listed case restricts the application of your case to specific, limited circumstances)
m	modified
o	overruled
p	parallel (this code means the listed case describes the case you are Shepardizing as "on all fours" with it; it finds your case directly on point in all respects)
q	questioned
r	reversed
S	superseded (as opposed to lowercase "s", which means the listed case is the "same case" as the case you are Shepardizing)
v	vacated

The codes appear prior to the Shepard's citation for the citing case. E.g., the listing "f 939P.2d894" means the case found at 939 P.2d 894 follows the opinion you are Shepardizing. The listing "d 345FS²616" means the case at 345 F. Supp. 616 distinguishes the case you are Shepardizing and does so regarding the point of law discussed in headnote 2 of the case (here, this refers to West's headnote from the printed report of the opinion). You do not know on what basis the court distinguished your case, or whether this is significant to your potential use of the case; it only alerts you that a later case has distinguished it.

As shown in the example above, "d 345FS616," Shepard's uses its own, non-Bluebook abbreviation for certain reporters. There is a table of such abbreviations at the beginning of each volume of Shepard's.

2.   Can Shepard's miss *negative* subsequent history?

Almost every reported case stands for one or more points of law. If a subsequent case overturns the **law** applied by your case by reversing, criticizing, limiting, or modifying one or more of the authorities upon which your case is relying, then the case you are researching may no longer be a good authority. The underpinning of your case may have been cut away. But this fact will not show up in Shepard's unless the subsequent case cites your case, and it may not. Therefore, just because your case checks out in Shepard's with a clean bill of health, it does not mean the law the case stands for (and therefore, the case itself) is still good law.

3.   How do you compensate for this?

Rarely will you have only one case in an area of law to Shepardize, so when you Shepardize the rest of your cases, the odds improve that any drastic changes wrought by subsequent cases will show up in the history of one or more of the cases you have found and are planning to rely on. Thus, generally you will be tipped off to any significant changes. Also, you are going to be doing other kinds of research—in digests, annotations, law reviews, treatises, perhaps even encyclopedias and legal periodicals—and any significant change in the law should be covered in those volumes as well. These kind of things are not kept a secret; however, do not live under the (risky) delusion that a clean check in Shepard's means the case is good as gold.

4.   Should the codes alone be enough to cause you to doubt a case?

The little codes Shepard's uses are very useful in flagging cases for you, but you must still read the cases! Maybe the subsequent case only overturned part of the opinion you want to use, leaving the part you like as "good law." Maybe it modified the case, but this modification does not affect your issue. Codes like "distinguished," "explained" don't tell you much—you must read the cases to find out what's going on (this goes for on-line verification, too).

Reliance on the codes alone one way or the other is fraught with peril. The Shepard's people are human and have been known to be wrong—they may list a case as "criticizing" your case, but when you read the case, you find that it does not criticize the case at all. The bottom line is that you are always ultimately responsible for your research. Saying that Shepard's said it was OK is akin to saying that the dog ate your homework.

5.   Shepard's for Non-Cases

Shepard's also exist for A.L.R. annotations, and for statutes, rules, administrative regulations, and constitutional provisions from the states and the federal system (e.g., Shepard's for the Code of Federal Regulations (C.F.R.), Federal Rules of Civil Procedure (Fed. R. Civ. P.), Internal Revenue code and certain IRS documentation, procedures and opinions). Shepard's are there for some "major" law reviews and the restatements of the law, and there are even Shepard's for patents, copyrights and trademarks.

Some Shepard's cover one particular subject matter (*e.g.*, Bankruptcy, Banking, Corporations, Criminal, Energy, Immigration, Labor, Occupational Safety and Health (OSHA), Insurance, Medical Malpractice, Partnership, Products Liability, Professional Conduct, Tax, Uniform Commercial Code (U.C.C.)).

A useful companion volume to Shepard's is <u>Shepard's Acts & Cases by Popular Names, Federal & State</u>. This references all state and federal laws by their "short title," a title that is featured with almost every statute and act (*e.g.*, Securities Act of 1933, Securities Exchange Act of 1934,

Clean Air Act). Citations are provided to the state statutes and session laws, federal statutes (U.S. Code), and federal Statutes at Large. The case part lists some famous (or notorious) cases by their popular names (The "Right to Life" case; the "Flag Burning Case").

6.   Which Shepard's do you use?

Shepard's comes in many forms:

State specific citators, which provide the official and parallel citations of citing cases from the state where the case arose (and only that one state).

Regional citators, for each of West's regional reporters, which give the regional reporter citations for each citing case, including cases from state and federal courts other than those in the state where the case arose.

Federal citators (for the Federal Reporter or the Federal Supplement) if you have a federal case; these will scour the nation for federal and state cases citing the federal case.

All Shepard's list A.L.R.s and law reviews (local ones, and the twenty or so "major" ones that Shepard's likes).

7.   Updating Shepard's

Updating Shepard's Citations volumes can be tedious because the printed volumes are not cumulative, *i.e.,* they do not repeat information previously printed by them. If your case is old, you will need to pull two or more hard bound volumes to run the history of your case. Shepard's does not use pocket parts to update their volumes; instead, there are softbound supplements and supplements to supplements. Hence, when you are running a history, each successive volume of Shepard's Citations must be consulted, from the "old" bound volumes to the "newer" bound volumes, through the interim paperback cumulations, to the most recent paperback update.

Shepard's does, however, give you a hint as to what volumes are needed to run a complete history of a certain case: the cover of the most recent supplement will tell you which volumes to consult to get the most up-to-date coverage. Thus, you will not have to search through a bunch of soft cover volumes that have been superseded and outdated (that your librarian hasn't gotten around to throwing away yet).

Part II – Reporters of cases

I.   FEDERAL AND STATE REPORTERS OF CASES

Your law school experience so far most likely has centered on your reading judicial opinions, because the "case method" of teaching the law remains overwhelmingly popular in the first year curriculum. In legal research as well, cases can define the law on any given topic by creating and advancing the law though the Common Law process of *stare decisis*, and by interpreting and modifying the law that is created through the other primary sources of legislation and administrative rules and regulations. Reporters, such as the Federal Reporter, New York Miscellaneous Reports, or Kentucky Reports, contain the opinions and orders of courts that you will study in order to determine the law.

You cannot talk about the reporting of cases in the United States without talking about West Publishing Company (or as it is currently known, Thomson Reuters, which now owns West). West publishes a report of the vast majority of cases that are issued in the United States. Along with the West publications, there are some states that have their own official reporter for the cases issued by the state's highest court or all of the courts in the state.

Part II of this chapter discusses reporters and the elements of reported cases and examines in detail the system for reporting cases used by West, including West's National Reporter system for state and federal cases. A handy tool to keep at your fingertips as we discuss this material is the Bluebook or the ALWD Citation Manual, which not only tell you how to cite to particular reporters, but also indicate which reporters are the "official" compilations for particular jurisdictions.

A.   Case reporters

1.   Case reports and reporters

Reporters are compilations of cases, most often organized by jurisdiction (*e.g.*, New York Reports, Illinois Reports, Federal Reporter), or by geography (North Eastern Reporter, South Western Reporter), or by subject matter (*e.g.*, Federal Securities Law Reporter; Employment Decisions, Federal Rules Decisions), or by year, or by some combination of the these categories (*e.g.*, year and subject matter).

2.   "Unpublished" cases

If a case is not published in an official outlet for a jurisdiction's cases—the official reporter for the jurisdiction or a supplemental or regional reporter—then the case is referred to as "unpublished" (remember, though, that does not automatically mean the case cannot be cited).

You will find unpublished opinions in the form of: (1) slip opinions, which are separate looseleaf pages put out by the court itself and picked up by attorneys, law firms, judge's chambers, and law offices (and may or may not ultimately be slated for publication); or (2) computerized versions of court opinions found in databases through computer assisted legal research. The primary on-line legal research providers, Lexis and Westlaw, pick up slip opinions and other copies of a court's opinions as they are issued by the court and they make them available on their on-line research databases regardless of whether the cases eventually will be put into a reporter. Occasionally, you can find unpublished opinions in loose-leaf publications on specific legal topics, such as the Securities Law Reporter, and the BNA Labor Law Reports. Although not published in an official outlet, these opinions are more readily available, even to lawyers who do not use computer-assisted legal research, and therefore, they carry more weight than other officially "unpublished" material unless the local rules of your jurisdiction specifically declare that commercially published cases still are "unpublished" and may not be used in official legal documents in that jurisdiction.

3.   State trial level court opinions

Opinions from state trial level courts generally are not published in print; they are available in much greater quantities through the on-line services of Westlaw and Lexis. There are exceptions to the print deficit, including trial level cases from New York, Pennsylvania, Virginia, and Ohio, which are regularly published in reporters. In contrast, in the federal system, many (although, increasingly, not all) opinions of the U.S. District Courts are published, and those that are published are found in the Federal Supplement reporter or the Federal Rules Decisions.

4.   Appellate level court opinions

Most state and federal reporters are devoted to publishing the reports of appellate level courts. These courts issue controlling authority, so it is particularly important for researchers to make themselves aware of the cases that the appellate courts of the applicable jurisdiction have issued on the topic of the research.

On occasion, appellate court judges decide not to publish a certain opinion. There are various reasons why this decision is made at the appellate level, such as: (1) the judges think the case does not involve significantly new legal principles and the law on this topic needs no further explanation or elucidation from the facts and issues involved in the case at hand; (2) the judges have determined to write a more cursory opinion in the case, often referred to as a ***per curiam*** opinion, which would be incomplete as a precedent if lawyers tried to use it in the future; (3) the judges have decided only to publish opinions that are highly topical or highly significant; or (4) the judges have decided to publish opinions only where they are making new law—changing, adding to, overruling, or modifying the law in some way. (In contrast, increasingly more trial level court opinions are available, but are not slated for publication).

5.   Reporting in two or more different reporters

"Parallel reporting" of cases is common in the United States. By publishing the same cases in a variety of outlets, the publishers attempt to make them available to a wider circle of researchers. For example, New York Court of Appeals opinions are reported in three different reporters—The New York Reports, the New York Supplement Reporter, and the North Eastern Reporter. U.S. Supreme Court cases are reported in the United States Reports, the Supreme Court Reporter, and the Lawyer's Edition Reporter. For citation purposes, it is important to know which reporter (or reporters) is considered the "official" one in your jurisdiction.

B.   Elements of Reported Opinions

1.   The caption (also called the title or style) of the case.

The parties' names are featured in the report of a judicial opinion, usually written as <u>Plaintiff's Name v. Defendant's Name</u>. Other forms are:

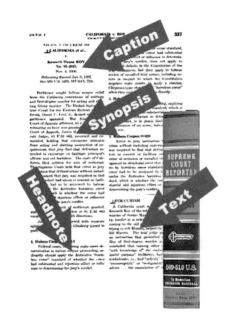

<u>In re Party's Name</u>

<u>State ex rel. Jay Nixon, Attorney General, v. Defendant</u>

<u>Ex Parte Party's Name</u>

<u>Plaintiff #1's Name v. Defendant #1's Name</u>
[where there are multiple plaintiffs and multiple defendants]

2.   The citation

Very often a citation to the case is given at the beginning of the case, and sometimes the report also gives the citation of the case in a different reporter—a "parallel citation." The citation is a shorthand reference to the reporter(s) where the case is found:

N.Y.; N.Y.2d—   New York Reports; New York Reports, Second Series

F.; F.2d; F.3d—   Federal Reporter; Federal Reporter, Second
                          Series; Federal Reporter, Third Series

The citation gives the volume number first, then the shorthand for
the reporter, then the page number where the case begins:

212 N.E.2d 43   Citation for a case in volume 212 of the
                          North Eastern Reporter, Second Series
                          beginning at p. 43.

788 F. Supp. 239   Citation for a case in volume 788 of the
                          Federal Supplement Reporter beginning
                          at p. 239.

Further information is required when you are citing the case in legal writing. Although the citations and parallel citations given in a reporter are useful, they do not necessarily correspond to proper Bluebook or
ALWD Manual citation forms. In fact, much of the time they are wrong.

3.   The court

A report of an opinion always discloses the court that issued the
opinion. The level of court and the court's place within or without the
applicable hierarchy of judicial authority will be of particular importance
to any researcher.

4.   Docket number

Usually, the report gives the docket number of the case. The docket number is the number assigned to the case by the clerk's office of the
court where the case was filed. The combination of numbers and letters
tells the informed reader certain information about the case, such as:

4:98-CV-455-DJS   In the U.S. District Court for the Eastern
                          District of Missouri, these numbers tell
                          you the case was filed in the Eastern
                          Division, it was filed in 1998, it was the
                          455th civil case filed in 1998, and it was
                          assigned to Judge Donald J. Stohr.

696-2487, Division 5   In the Missouri Circuit Court for the 22nd Judicial Circuit, these numbers tell you that this case was filed in St. Louis City in 1996, it was the 2,487th case filed that year, and that it was assigned to Division 5 of the court.

5.   Date of the decision and opinion

As discussed in Chapter 5, the dates of the opinions are very important to the ranking of the authorities as legal precedent. More recent authority generally is stronger than earlier authority if all else is equal.

6.   Synopsis (a/k/a prefatory statement, heading, summary)

Sometimes the first text printed in a case report is a short paragraph summarizing the case, informing the reader which party prevailed in the case, and giving a little background information about the facts and issues involved in the case. If this paragraph appears before the judge's name, then it is **not** part of the actual opinion. The publisher of the case reporter—and not the court—wrote it and inserted it into the report of the case. The publisher is giving the reader a brief introduction to the case, which is helpful for the reader to use to orient herself. **However, because it is not part of the actual opinion, you should not cite to it!** It is also advisable to read the synopsis critically and not simply rely on what it says about the case because every once in a while the publishers of these summaries have been known to get the information about the issues or the holding of the case wrong. Even if it isn't "wrong" it may not articulate the law in a way that is the most beneficial or productive for your needs.

If a paragraph summarizing the case appears below the judge's name in the body of the opinion, then it is part of the opinion, and you can cite to it and rely on what it says. In these instances, it should be called an introductory section rather than a synopsis, heading, or summary.

7.   Headnotes and syllabi

Reporters published by West all have headnotes. Other publishers also write syllabi or headnotes at the start of their opinions. Headnotes and syllabi are short paragraphs that break out the individual legal principles that were discussed in the case. They can serve as thumbnail sketches of some or all of the legal issues that were taken up by the court in the opinion and what the court said about them.

Headnotes and syllabi are *always* printed before the judge's name and before the body of the opinion, so they are **not** part of the actual opinion. **Therefore, you should not cite to them, and as with synopses and summaries, you should read them critically and not automatically rely on what they say about the legal principles discussed in the case.** Headnotes and syllabi are the creation of the editorial staff of the publisher, not the court that issued the opinion, and the publisher may have interpreted the case incorrectly or in a way that limits its utility for your purposes.

West's headnotes not only give a thumbnail sketch of the various issues involved in a single case, but the headnotes themselves are collected and republished in other volumes called **digests** (also published by West), where they are categorized and organized by the general area of law, subtopic in that area, and specific issue or "key words" within the area of law. This collection and organization is one of the greatest benefits of the West system and its utility should not be underestimated. Digests are a great resource to find cases that are on point for your legal research.

8.   Names of counsel

The names of the attorneys who represented the parties in the case sometimes are printed in the case.

9.   Facts

Rarely is there a separate "statement of facts" section identified as such in an opinion. It is customary for the court to discuss the facts up front, but often this fact section simply will be the first three or four paragraphs of the body of the opinion, with no obvious separation from the rest of the opinion. The court can bring up and discuss new facts at any time in the case, and a careful reader will watch out for these new facts. The facts discussed are part of the opinion, and you can cite to them and rely on them in your analysis just like any other part of the opinion.

10. Opinions of the court and separate opinions of judges

The author of the opinion is printed just above the body of the opinion. With multi-judge courts, there are a number of possible combinations of judges who sign off on the opinion or who write their own opinion in the case:

Unanimous opinion	Every judge votes the same way.
En banc opinion	The whole court or a large number of judges on the court sat to hear the case— Note well that only a majority of the judges on the court, not all of the judges, have to agree in order for the opinion to be called an *en banc* opinion with the additional force and weight that this designation carries.
Majority opinion	A numeric majority of the judges that heard the case—2 out of 3, 3 out of 5, 5 out of 9, 7 out of 12—agreed with the opinion.
Plurality opinion	There was no single opinion commanding a numeric majority, but one opinion (the plurality opinion) got more votes than any other separate opinion, and a majority of the judges or justices agreed with the outcome reflected in that opinion although not with its rationale. For example, in the U.S. Supreme Court with its nine justices, a plurality opinion might have received four votes, two other judges might have concurred in the result, and there may have

been one or more dissenting opinions, none of which received as many as four votes.

Concurring opinion   One or more judges agree with the end result of a majority or plurality opinion, but the judges want to express different reasons as to why they think this result should be reached.

Dissenting opinion   One or more judges do not agree with the majority opinion or the plurality opinion, and they write separately to express how they think the case should be resolved.

Per Curiam opinion   An opinion of the entire panel in which no particular judge of the panel is identified as the "author." Often it is more cursory and less detailed in its discussion of the facts and the law than other opinions of the court, and often the judges will withhold it from official publication.

11.   Decision—the judgment, order, or decree

The judgment declares who won and who lost. It will order or award relief to one or more parties, or it will affirm, reverse, or remand the case at hand.

C.   Official and Unofficial Reporters

Every jurisdiction has at least one "official" reporter for the jurisdiction's judicial opinions that are to be published, whether they are from the jurisdiction's appellate courts or trial level courts or both. Some jurisdictions have several "unofficial" reporters where the same opinions (and sometimes others) also can be published. To make matters worse, some jurisdictions used to have an official reporter, and then they abandoned it, and some previously unofficial reporter became the only reporter of that jurisdiction's case, and thus was transformed into the "official reporter."

New York, Illinois, and California have an "official" reporter—the New York Reports, the Illinois Reports, and the California Reports. They have an unofficial regional reporter, West's North Eastern Reporter encompassing New York and Illinois, and the Pacific Reporter encompassing California. In addition, they each have a second unofficial reporter, West's New York Supplement reporter, West's Illinois Decisions reporter, and West's California Reporter. Missouri falls into the category of states that used to have an "official" reporter—the Missouri Reports for the Missouri Supreme Court's cases— but it is now defunct, and the Missouri Supreme Court's cases are published in West's regional reporter encompassing Missouri, called the South Western Reporter. Thus, the South Western Reporter now is Missouri's "official" reporter.

The Bluebook (or ALWD Manual) tells you which reporters are "official" and which are "unofficial" for each of the states. When you are writing something to a court in a state, the Bluebook requires you to follow local rules, which often require you to cite to the "official" reporter in that state and to provide a parallel citation to each of the unofficial reporters (if any exist in that state, and if the case is found therein). Otherwise, when referring to a state's opinions in a memorandum or in a document prepared for a lawsuit pending in a different state, you can cite to an unofficial reporter—usually the West regional reporter for that state.

II. REPORTERS OF FEDERAL COURT CASES

The following section discusses the reporters of **federal cases** and the official citation form for each of the reporters.

A. United States Supreme Court cases

1. Official Reporter: The United States Reports (U.S.)

2. Unofficial Reporters: Supreme Court Reporter (S. Ct.)

                                  Lawyer's Edition Reporter (L.
                                  Ed., L. Ed. 2d)

3. Other: United States Law Week
                                  (U.S.L.W.) unofficial, advance
                                  reports of cases

The earlier official volumes of the U.S. Supreme Court cases (up to 1874) were organized and identified by the name of the reporter who collected the cases and published them in volumes; e.g., Cranch, Black, Wallace. Later they were re-organized into volumes 1-90 of the U.S. Reports, but the official citation to these cases still includes the reporter's name. For example:

14 U.S. (1 Wheat.) 15, 18 (1816)

5 U.S. (1 Cranch) 101, 104-05 (1801)

The Bluebook requires you to cite to the United States reports (U.S.) if the case is published therein. If it is not yet in the U.S. Reports (it does take a year or more for the Government Printing Office to get each volume organized and published) then you cite to the case in other volumes in this order of preference: cite to the Supreme Court Reporter (S. Ct.) first, but if it is not in there, cite to the Lawyer's Edition (L. Ed., L. Ed. 2d), and if not even there, then cite to the U.S. Law Week (U.S.L.W.).

B.   Federal court of appeals cases

The opinions of the United States Courts of Appeals (1881-present) are reported in one official reporter—the **Federal Reporter (F., F.2d, F.3d)**. There are no unofficial reporters, but some are "unpublished" and found only as slip opinions or on Lexis and Westlaw. The citation forms look like this:

Greenbaum v. Greenhaw, 112 F.3d 234, 235 (8th Cir. 1998) [regular citation]

Murray v. Griggs, No. 97-2346-EDM, ___ F.3d ___, 1998 WL 12567, at *4 (8th Cir. Nov. 23, 1998) [Note the docket number and the long form of the date. This citation indicates that the case will be published in the Federal Reporter eventually, but it hasn't made it there yet—for now, you can find it on Westlaw, and you are referring to page *4 of the opinion]

Kelley v. Underwood, No. 95-1234-WDM, 1996 WL 12778, at *5 (8th Cir. Jan. 14, 1996) [This indicates that the case was not and will not be published in the Federal Reporter—but you can find it on Westlaw, and the citation is to p. *5 of the case]

Goldman v. Weinberger, No. 95 Civ. 1245, slip op. at 5 (9th Cir. Jun. 22, 1996) [The case only exists as a slip opinion—here you are citing to page 5 of the slip opinion]

Earlier U.S. Courts of Appeals' opinions (1789-1880) were compiled and published in volumes called **Federal Cases (F. Cas.)**, arranged not by year but alphabetically. There are tables to help you locate cases when you only know the year and one party for example. Each case is numbered sequentially, and the proper citation to these cases includes the sequential number as follows:

Delrich v. Pittsburgh, 18 F. Cas. 598, 602 (C.C.W.D. Pa. 1859) (No. 10,444).

C.   Federal district court cases

The opinions of the United States District Courts (1932-present), to the extent they are published, are reported in one official reporter— the **Federal Supplement (F. Supp., F. Supp. 2d).** Note the space between the F. and the Supp. in the citation short form. There are no unofficial reporters, but many opinions are unreported and found as slip opinions or on Lexis and Westlaw.

Baum v. Green, 998 F. Supp. 134, 138-39 (E.D. Mo. 1997) [regular citation]

DeSanctis v. Gruggs, No. 4:97-CV-2346-DJS, ___ F. Supp. ___, 1998 WL 18367, at *2 (N.D.N.C. Nov. 23, 1998) [Note the docket number and the long form of the date. This citation indicates that the case will be published in the Federal Supplement eventually, but it hasn't made it there yet—for now, you can find it on Westlaw, and you are citing to page *2 of the opinion]

Kelley v. Underwood, No. 95CV1234WS, 1996 WL 17998, at *3 (S.D. Ill. Jan. 14, 1996) [This indicates that the case was not and will not be published in the Federal Supplement—but you can find it on Westlaw, and *3 is the page number you are referring to]

Vermeil v. The St. Louis Rams Football Club, No. 695 Civ. 1245, slip op. at 5 (W.D. Mo. Jun. 24, 1996) [The case only exists as a slip opinion—here you are citing to page 5 of the slip opinion]

Earlier opinions (pre-1932) of the U.S. District Courts, to the extent they were published, were published in the Federal Reporter. Certain U.S. District Court cases that construe, interpret and apply the Federal Rules of Civil Procedure (Fed. R. Civ. P.) and the Federal Rules of Criminal Procedure (Fed. R. Crim. P.) are reported in the **Federal Rules Decisions (F.R.D.)**. Cases reported in the Federal Rules Decisions are not reported in the Federal Supplement volumes. The reason that the Federal Rules Decisions exists is that federal trial level courts are the only courts that deal with the Federal Rules of Civil and Criminal Procedure on a day-to-day basis (because these rules have to do with litigation and trials), so they have much more occasion to interpret and apply these rules and their opinions on the rules carry more weight than the average U.S. District Court opinion. A citation to the Federal Rules Decisions appears as follows:

Dole v. Clinton, 188 F.R.D. 144, 152 (N.D. Cal. 1997)

D.   Other volumes for federal cases

1. **Military Justice Reporter (M.J.)** - reports appeals from military court martials.

2. **Bankruptcy Reporter (B.R.)** - reports bankruptcy law decisions from the U.S. Bankruptcy Courts and the U.S. District Courts and reprints certain U.S. Supreme Court and U.S. Court of Appeals' decisions on bankruptcy law.

3. **Federal Claims Reporter (Fed. Cl.)** - reports opinions from the U.S. Claims Court which is a trial level federal court that hears claims against the United States, usually arising from a government contract.

III.   REPORTERS OF STATE COURT CASES

The following are examples of reporters for state cases, and their proper citation form:

A.   Official reporters

An official reporter is the reporter specifically designated by the state to report the state's cases. There may be an official reporter for each level of court in the state, or one reporter that reports all the appellate courts in the state.

Example: New York Reports (N.Y., N.Y.2d) – reports New York Court of Appeals cases.

N.Y. Appellate Division Reports (A.D., A.D.2d) – reports New York Supreme Court Appellate Division cases.

Illinois Reports (Ill., Ill. 2d) – reports Illinois Supreme Court cases.

Illinois Appellate Court Reports (Ill. App., Ill. App. 2d) – reports Illinois Appellate Court cases.

Idaho Reports (Idaho) – reports both Idaho Supreme Court and Idaho Court of Appeals cases.

If the state's name (*e.g.*, Alaska or Idaho) or a two, three or four letter abbreviation for the state (*e.g.*, Kan., Mass., Md., Mich.) is given by itself as the shorthand for a reporter, it reports the state's highest court's opinions. Idaho, Kan., Mass., Md., Mich. are the abbreviations for the official reporters of the courts of last resort in Idaho, Kansas, Massachusetts, Maryland, and Michigan. In some instances, as with Idaho above, this reporter also will report intermediate level appellate court cases.

If an "App." is put next to the state's short abbreviation, this becomes the abbreviation for a reporter that reports the state's intermediate level appellate court's opinions. E.g., Cal. App., Cal. App. 2d—reports the California Court of Appeal's opinions.

B.   Regional reporters—official and unofficial

National Reporter System Map
showing the states included in each reporter

West's Regional Reporters have divided the country into unusual geographical regions. Illinois is in the region covered by the North Eastern Reporter (N.E., N.E.2d), Kentucky and Missouri are in the region covered by the South Western Reporter (S.W., S.W.2d), Iowa is in the region covered by the North Western Reporter (N.W., N.W.2d), and Kansas is in the region covered by the Pacific Reporter (P., P.2d). West's regional reporters generally are unofficial reporters of state court cases, but many exceptions exist. For example, the South Western Reporter is the official reporter of Missouri's cases, but it is an unofficial reporter of Arkansas's cases.

When citing a case that is reported in a regional reporter, you must tell the reader where the opinion originated. This information is enclosed in parentheses before the year of the opinion. Similar rules apply for short abbreviations as with official reporters above—if the abbreviation for the state is given by itself, it stands for the state's highest court. If some version of "App." appears next to it,

it stands for the intermediate level appellate court. For example:

> Bell v. Jar, 887 So. 2d 334 (Ala. 1992) [highest level court in Alabama—the Alabama Supreme Court]

> Hoe v. Rake, 788 S.W.2d 332 (Mo. Ct. App. E. Dist. 1992) [intermediate level appellate court—the Missouri Court of Appeals, Eastern District]

> Johns v. Con Edison Corp., 45 N.E.2d 23 (N.Y. 1951) [highest level court in New York—the New York Court of Appeals]

> Rivera v. C.B.C., Inc., 324 N.E.2d 479 (N.Y. App. Div. 3d Dep't 1963) [intermediate level appellate court—the New York Appellate Division, Third Department]

C.   West's state-specific publications

Some states have a special West reporter devoted solely to that state's cases. As you might guess, the states with the biggest population and the most potential for lawsuits get this treatment. Examples:

New York Supplement (N.Y.S., N.Y.S.2d. N.Y.S.3d)

Illinois Decisions (Ill. Dec.)

California Reporter (Cal. Rptr., Cal. Rptr. 2d. Cal. Rptr. 3d)

D.   West's reprint editions of one state's cases

As a convenience to practitioners with more limited budgets, West often will reprint one state's cases that are taken out of the regional reporter where these cases originally were published. These volumes are given a name on the spine, such as "Colorado Cases," or "Texas Cases," but these are not a separate state-specific reporter, as discussed in the section above. These volumes maintain the same volume and page numbers as the regional reporters where the cases originally were published, so you would cite to the regional reporter as if that is the volume where you found the particular case you are researching. For example, when citing a Colorado case that you found in "Colorado Cases," you still would cite the volume and page number from Pacific Reporter where the case originally was published, not the "Colorado Cases" reprint reporter. **Do not attempt to cite the reprint volume, not even as a parallel citation.**

E.   Topical, subject matter reporters

There are private publishers other than West that publish (or in most cases, republish) cases that deal with a single specific area of the law. Practitioners of that area of the law may subscribe to the reporters so that they can keep a more limited number of volumes on their shelves that still will contain the cases they will need to turn to time and time again. Examples of these reporters and their citation forms are as follows:

The Blue Sky Law Reports (Blue Sky L. Rep.) (CCH)—reports state securities law cases. [Note: the separate parentheses in the citation that gives the shorthand for the private publisher, Commerce Clearing House].

Environmental Reporter Cases (Env't Rep. Cas.) (BNA)—prints environmental law case. [BNA indicates a private publisher, the Bureau of National Affairs].

IV.   WEST'S NATIONAL REPORTER SYSTEM

The Supreme Court Reporter, Federal Reporter, Federal Supplement, and all the regional reporters make up West's National Reporter System. West collects and publishes all fifty states' opinions and the federal courts' opinions in various reporter series, all following  the West model of annotating and categorizing the opinions.

Each reporter in the system follows the West model for reporting cases, and has the following components:

1. **Introduction, synopsis**—all West cases have this introductory section at the start of each case. It is written by West, not the court, and it is not part of the opinion and should not be cited. Occasionally, the editors who draft these sections get the information wrong. They may erroneously report who won, or misstate the outcome of certain issues, so you always should double-check the opinion itself before using any information found in the synopsis.

2. **Headnotes (a/k/a Key Notes)**—West writes headnotes for the various issues of law that are taken up by the opinion. Lists of headnotes from cases are categorized and compiled into digests based on topical key numbers. You can research in the digests for specific topics and key numbers to find cases that have discussed that specific legal issue. Again, these headnotes are not part of the opinion, so do not cite to them. As with the synopsis, headnotes can report things erroneously, so always check the information against the text of the opinion itself.

3. **Advance sheets**—West prints preliminary editions of their case reports in paperback form, and they print these volumes soon after the cases are issued and far in advance of the cases' publication in "official" government operated reporters. The cases reported in the advance sheets already are assigned their permanent volume and page number, which does not change when they are put in a hard-bound edition of the West reporter. Your cites to a West advance sheet still will be accurate when the cases in the advance sheets are converted to a hardbound volume.

4. **Reference Aids**—West generates Tables of Cases, cross-references to the official reporters' citations, statutes construed, rules construed, a mini-digest just for each reporter volume, lists of judges for each court reported in the volume, and many more reference aids. The advance sheets also have "Judicial Highlights" and "Congressional and Administrative Highlights" which are reports of recent cases and recently enacted laws and administrative rules and regulations.

Chapter 4

Researching Federal Regulatory and Administrative Law

This Chapter provides a basic overview of how to research a rather complicated but extremely important topic – especially if you plan to work in a highly regulated field, such as environmental law, energy law, or telecommunications law. The interplay among the legislative and executive branches raises important separation of powers questions, and researching matters implicating highly regulated industries can mean getting your hands dirty with extremely technical issues. We highly recommend that you consider taking a course in Administrative Law if you really want to master this subject matter area and further contextualize the research methods discussed below.

I. WHY REGULATORY AND ADMINISTRATIVE FUNCTIONS ARE DELEGATED BY CONGRESS AND THE EXECUTIVE BRANCH

Members of Congress and other government officials recognize that they cannot regulate every area of conduct in the modern world by passing new laws or amending old ones. They do not have the time, certain areas are too complex and detailed with minutia to allow effective legislative drafting, and certain areas are simply beyond their expertise to regulate. Similarly, they recognize that a piece of legislation cannot feasibly account for every situation that may arise when the law is applied to particular circumstances or behaviors.

Thus, the power to regulate certain areas is delegated to administrative and regulatory agencies and commissions. Congress can choose an existing agency to take on the task, or in rarer circumstances, it can create and fund an entirely new agency or commission to assume the task.

The delegation itself occurs through a broadly worded **statute** setting out the intention to regulate an area, along with a specific reference to implementation by regulations, and specific delegation to an agency or commission. The Executive Branch (the President, the Cabinet Departments of government) can also delegate this rule-making and regulatory authority to agencies through an **Executive Order**.

Executive and judicial powers often are delegated to the agency—thus, the power to make rules and regulations often coincides with the power to adjudicate disputes arising under the laws that the agency is charged with executing and administrating. For example, the Securities Exchange Commission can prosecute and adjudicate claims and charges (administrative actions) under the federal securities laws as well as promulgate rules for the conduct of the securities business. The SEC also reviews applications and grants or withholds permission for certain actions that are undertaken in the business, such as an initial public offering by a formerly privately held business.

II.   TYPES OF ADMINISTRATIVE LAW

This chapter focuses on federal administrative rules and regulations, but there certainly are other forms of administrative laws:

1. **Orders**—reports of disposition and resolution of agency matters;

2. **Licenses and permits, certificates**, and other forms of permission or qualification;

3. **Advisory Opinions**—a report and advice concerning what the agency would do with a hypothetical situation. Often persons request the issuance of such an opinion so that they can see what the agency would do with their case. Agency opinions are considered to be a reliable and persuasive source for predicting the agency's behavior, but they are not binding on the agency and they are not binding on courts considering the same issue of law;

FYI

Why aren't advisory opinions and no-action letters binding on the administrative agency that issued them? The answer comes from two sources, one fairly complicated, the other fairly simple. The complicated explanation is that a hypothetical situation is not justiciable. The facts are not ripe for review, *i.e.*, the case or controversy may not yet have gelled. A final, reliable, enforceable judgment cannot be entered. This leads to the simple explanation: the agency wants to be helpful and agrees to answer hypothetical questions, but it doesn't want its hands to be tied by an opinion based on hypothetical facts when it later must rule on an actual case or controversy with complete, concrete facts.

4. **No-Action Letters**—specific to certain areas, such as securities regulation, these are opinions of the agency on a specific set of facts indicating that the agency will not take any action against the party requesting the No-Action Letter. The party requesting the letter can rely on the promise of no action. Others may attempt to use the No-Action Letter as persuasive authority in a subsequent agency action or a court proceeding as proof that the law should be enforced the same way in similar situations (akin to Advisory Opinions, above), but the letters are not binding on the agency in other parties' cases and they are not binding on the courts;

5. **Decisions**—reports of the agency's rulings in an administrative and regulatory action concerning a party accused of violating the rules and regulations of the agency. These decisions arise through adjudicatory functions. The actual prosecution by the agency is separate from the adjudication, the latter function being performed by special boards of review, administrative law judges, hearing examiners, or other officers, so that the same persons are not prosecutor, judge, and jury. These decisions are used as precedent in later cases, and are considered highly persuasive although they are not binding on the agency or the courts.

III.   THE FEDERAL REGISTER

Once the authority to regulate is delegated, the agencies charged with rule-making responsibilities are empowered to institute rules—also called "regulations"—which have the full force and effect of law on the public as if Congress itself had enacted them. The agency must implement their regulations in the proper fashion; *i.e.*, in accordance with the Administrative Procedures Act, 5 U.S.C. §§ 553 *et seq.* and §§ 701 *et seq.*

The Administrative Procedures Act is a critical text for anyone whose practice area involves highly regulated industries. In essence, it provides that administrative rules must follow certain procedures for public notice of their proposal, namely, issuance of "proposed rules," with opportunity for public comment and input and, ultimately, publication as a "Final Rule" for all to see. To this end, the Federal Register ("Fed. Reg.") was established. It is published daily by the U.S. Government Printing Office every day that the federal government is in operation. **See http://www.gpo.gov/.**

The Federal Register – available and searchable for free online through the GPO at http://www.gpoaccess.gov/fr/index.html -- is the vehicle by which the public is notified that certain rules or regulations, or modifications of the same are under consideration, and where the public gets actual notice of applicable rules. The Code of Federal Regulations (CFR) is the publication where *all* final federal regulations are compiled and printed. See http://www.gpoaccess.gov/cfr/index.html (also searchable for free). The CFR, discussed in more detail below, works in tandem with the U.S. Code in that it contains all the regulations that have been promulgated in support of the various laws codified in the U.S. Code.

FYI

The Library of Congress also has a website - http://thomas.loc.gov/ -- that allows you to search a variety of government-related texts and resources. THOMAS was launched in January of 1995, at the inception of the 104th Congress. The leadership of the 104th Congress directed the Library of Congress to make federal legislative information freely available to the public. Since that time THOMAS has expanded the scope of its offerings to include coverage of the following (a non-exhaustive list):

- Bills and Resolutions (current and past)

- Activity in Congress

- The Congressional Record

- Committee Information

- Presidential Nominations

- Treaties

It is worth surfing around on the THOMAS website to get yourself oriented with its vast resources. It's another *free* research source, and you may find (once you get used to its layout) that you can locate information there as easily as you can via a paid service, and you may even just find some really interesting stuff.

Each issue of the Federal Register may contain:

- Table of Contents listing the agencies reporting in the issue and page references to the various items associated with these agencies;

- CFR Parts Affected in this Issue (see Updating, below);

- Presidential Documents;

- Proposed Rules—allowing the public to comment on same;

- Notices—reports other than rules, regulations and proposed rules; e.g., grant application deadlines, filing of petitions and applications;

- Sunshine Act Meetings;

- Unified Agenda of Federal Regulations—by virtue of the Regulatory Flexibility Act, in April and October the agencies publish an agenda of the regulatory actions they are proposing and developing. Rules appear in four groups: (1) Prerule stage; (2) Proposed Rule stage; (3) Final Rule stage; (4) Completed Actions;

- Reader Aids—phone numbers of who to contact for info; a **cumulative table of CFR Parts affected during the month**; parallel table of Fed. Reg. pages for the month; bills of Congress that recently have become law; and, on Mondays, a CFR Checklist of the CFR Parts;

- Special Sections—for publication of agency documents.

While the Federal Register is a nice open forum for comment and criticism, you would have to read the Federal Register every day to hope to stay on top of the rules in your area of the law and to find out if they were changed in some way; *i.e.*, were they amended or modified, superseded, or withdrawn. The Federal Register works like the Statutes at Large—it is a chronological, *newspaper-like* presentation of federal regulations, daily issue after issue piled one upon the other in an increasing flood of rules and regs—and you have heard how hard it is to stay on top of federal legislation just by reading the chronological output in the Statutes at Large.

Accessing the Federal Register has gotten a whole lot simpler since 1994, when the U.S. Government Printing Office (GPO) put a searchable version of the Federal Register on-line on its web site: http://www.gpoaccess.gov, as noted above. The GPO permits searches of the Federal Register (1994 forward) as well as the current edition of the Code of Federal Regulations (discussed below) *for free.* The GPO calls this "browsing," but it works like a regular Internet search. The results are sorted statistically by number of occurrences and proximity of your search terms.

Outside cyberspace, the Federal Register has a monthly index (the **Federal Register Index**), updated cumulatively each month, so that the December issue basically is an annual index of the year's rules and regulations. It lists rules alphabetically by agency rather than by subject matter, so you have to be up on which agency would be handling your topic.

Congressional Information Service publishes a **CIS Federal Regis-**

ter Index starting in 1984, issued weekly in loose-leaf form, with monthly cumulative indices and permanent semi-annual bound volumes. It has subject matter organization as well as cross-indexing by name, CFR sections affected, federal agency docket numbers, and a Calendar of Effective Dates and Comment Deadlines.

IV.   CODE OF FEDERAL REGULATIONS

The "Code of Federal Regulations" (CFR) was created to present a "codification" of the rules and regulations promulgated by the federal administrative agencies. CFR annually publishes only those rules and regulations that are in full force and effect at the time of its publication, and it is published (or re-published) in full once each year. Modified and withdrawn regulations are removed and the new ones or modified versions are published. Also omitted from the CFR is all the "legislative/rule-making history" information that preceded the final rule's publication, but which was printed in Federal Register. Perhaps most importantly, the CFR reorganizes the Federal Register's provisions into a subject organization.

In the same sense that Congressional hearings and reports and floor debates may be used in construing a statute's meaning, the "regulatory" or "rule-making" history may be used in divining a regulation's meaning and intent. The discussions, "preambles," interim reports, alternative suggestions, and other information remain buried in the Federal Register, and a researcher may need to dig them out to fully understand a provision. Fortunately, both the CFR and Federal Register provide useful "history" paragraphs with each provision that assist in this mining process.

The CFR's subject matter organization <u>roughly</u> parallels the subjects used in the United States Code. For example, Title 26 of the U.S. Code deals with federal taxation and the Internal Revenue Code and, similarly, 26 C.F.R. concerns the Internal Revenue Service and I.R.S. Regulations; Title 18 of the U.S. Code concerns the federal penal code and Code of Criminal Procedure and, similarly, 18 C.F.R. concerns the Justice Department and its operations and policies. But the parallelism between the respective subjects or "Titles" is not complete; <u>e.g.</u>, 17 C.F.R. deals with Commodities and Securities Regulation (which is Title 15 of the U.S.C.), not with copyright (Title 17 of the U.S. Code). Only 28 of the C.F.R.'s titles are the same as the U.S. Code's.

Within each CFR, the organization of the sections and subsections bears no similarity to the organization of the sections of the parallel U.S. Code titles, although they sometimes parallel the original legislation's organization (the organization found in the Statutes at Large) before the law was codified in the U.S. Code; e.g., Section 10(b) of the statutory text of the Securities Exchange Act of 1934 is implemented by 17 C.F.R. § 240.10b, while the codification of Section 10(b) is found at 15 U.S.C. § 78j.

A.   C.F.R.'s organization

The CFR is re-published annually, each time dropping out any regulation that has been withdrawn, or updating old provisions that were amended since the last CFR. edition. But the C.F.R. is published in four parts—one quarter of the text is published each calendar quarter. The first quarter (CFR Titles 1-16) is published on January 1st, the second quarter (CFR Titles 17-27) on April 1st, the third quarter (CFR Titles 28-41) on July 1st, and the last quarter (CFR Titles 42-50) on October 1st. Each quarterly set changes the color of the binding as the year passes, and the colors used change each year.

Whenever using a CFR volume, check its cover to see when that volume originated—that's when your "updating" problem will begin (see Subsection D below).

B.   Locating relevant and current C.F.R. provisions online

1.   Westlaw and Lexis

The Westlaw and Lexis CFR databases can be searched for regulations using key words (search terms). If you are in a statutory database, you can use the links to CFR sections listed in the annotations. The following illustrates the process on Westlaw using the example of 15 U.S.C. § 78j, which is the codification of section 10 of the Securities Exchange Act of 1934 dealing with manipulative and deceptive devices in the sale of securities, and its famous subsection 10(b) (15 U.S.C. § 78j(b)) dealing with securities fraud.

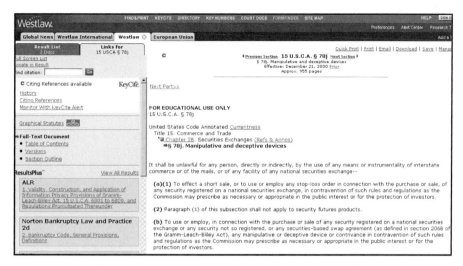

In the left column, if you scroll down you will find the links to the administrative law promulgated under this section:

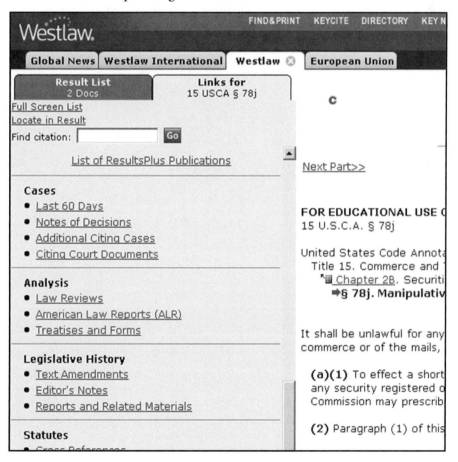

The link for administrative code produces a listing of the Code of Federal Regulations provisions associated with this provision:

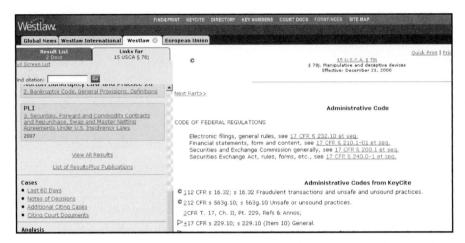

One of the rules promulgated under this section is Rule 10b-5 (17 C.F.R. 240.10b-5), which you will find by clinking on the Securities Exchange Act, rules, forms, etc. link shown above and browsing through the many provisions in 17 C.F.R. § 240:

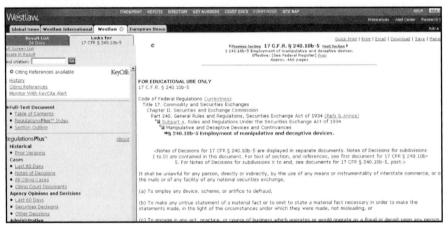

Here, KeyCite is available to see a list of citing references to Rule 10b-5 (all 29,861 of them):

You can search directly for C.F.R. provisions through the CFR database on Westlaw:

Or you can search in the Federal Register (FR) database:

2. Internet – www.gpoaccess.gov

The U.S. Government Printing Office will allow you to search the current edition of the CFR for free at its web site: http://www.gpoaccess.gov. As mentioned above, the site is searchable—the GPO calls it "browsing"—but it works like a regular Internet search. The results are

sorted statistically by number of occurrences and proximity of your search terms.

The link for Code of Federal Regulations brings up the search screen:

Here, you can do a quick search or click on the "Browse and/or Search the CFR" link which brings up a new page:

- To search or browse a **single** CFR Title for a given year, click on the desired revision date for that Title in the table below.
- *or -*
- To search or browse **one or more** CFR Titles, click the appropriate checkbox(es) in the table below, then click CONTINUE.

CONTINUE   CLEAR

Available CFR Titles on *GPO Access*														
Title	**Revision Date**													
	(Unless noted, all parts for a given Title are available)													
	2009	2008	2007	2006	2005	2004	2003	2002	2001	2000	1999	1998	1997	1996
1 General Provisions	Jan. 1, 2009	☐ Jan. 1, 2008	☐ Jan. 1, 2007	☐ Jan. 1, 2006	☐ Jan. 1, 2005	☐ Jan. 1, 2004	☐ Jan. 1, 2003	☐ Jan. 1, 2002	☐ Jan. 1, 2001	☐ Jan. 1, 2000	☐ Jan. 1, 1999	☐ Jan. 1, 1998	☐ Jan. 1, 1997	
2 Grants and Agreements	Jan. 1, 2009	☐ Jan. 1, 2008	☐ Jan. 1, 2007	☐ Jan. 1, 2006	Jan. 1, 2005									
3 The President	Jan. 1, 2009	☐ Jan. 1, 2008 Parts 100-102	☐ Jan. 1, 2007 Parts 100-102	☐ Jan. 1, 2006	☐ Jan. 1, 2005	☐ Jan. 1, 2004	☐ Jan. 1, 2003	☐ Jan. 1, 2002	☐ Jan. 1, 2001	☐ Jan. 1, 2000	☐ Jan. 1, 1999	☐ Jan. 1, 1998	☐ Jan. 1, 1997	
4 Accounts	Jan. 1, 2009	☐ Jan. 1, 2008	Jan. 1, 2007	☐ Jan. 1, 2006	☐ Jan. 1, 2005	☐ Jan. 1, 2004	☐ Jan. 1, 2003	☐ Jan. 1, 2002	☐ Jan. 1, 2001	☐ Jan. 1, 2000	☐ Jan. 1, 1999	☐ Jan. 1, 1998	☐ Jan. 1, 1997	

Here, you can explore whole titles of the Code of Federal Regulations.

Congressional Universe's web service contains the Federal Register from 1980 forward, and the current CFR, searchable for a fee (unless you use your academic license, or go through your local law library's system). The LEGI-SLATE service can be accessed on the Internet and you can search for Federal Register and CFR provisions. It is a fee based service. Counterpoint Publishing's web service contains the Federal Register from 1993 forward, and the current CFR—both are searchable for a fee.

C.   Locating relevant and current CFR provisions by the book

The CFR is indexed, but the index is nearly useless. The problem is the C.F.R. Index's subjects are determined by the literal nomenclature (titles) of the rules and regulations themselves, not by logical legal topics and subtopics. This is not how we (the average researchers) normally think of the law, and it is directly contrary to the methodology used by digests, encyclopedias, and dictionaries, and most legal indices. We should have no reason to expect that we can guess how <u>all</u> the relevant regulations for our area are going to be described. If there happens to be a rule or regulation with a title that matches what you are looking for, you will find it in the CFR index; but if you are searching for a topic not found in any title or description of a rule or regulation, you are out of luck. Therefore, almost any method of identifying relevant CFR provisions is superior to the CFR index.

Instead, use the implementing statutory authority that authorized and delegated the area. Annotated statutes, such as West's United States Code Annotated ("U.S.C.A.") and former Lawyers Coop's United States Code Service ("U.S.C.S.") annotate the U.S. Code provisions with references to regulations that those U.S. Code provisions spawn.

In addition, you can find regulations because they are discussed and cited in case law, law review articles, treatises, loose-leaf services and other specialty publications. The reference to relevant CFR provisions is general case law or journal databases is more hit or miss—not the start and end of good research into the applicable regulatory law—but you sometimes "hit" on a cite to a regulation in a case or law review article when you were not thinking about the CFR or possible regulations at all. However, it will usually be more effective to consult a good treatise or set of loose-leaf volumes devoted to the area you are researching, because these will specifically focus on the regulations in the area.

D.   Updating CFR provisions

Updating the actual content of regulations on Westlaw and Lexis or on the GPO Access site is unnecessary: the sites themselves are current. KeyCite on Westlaw will further alert you to proposed changes and rule-making. The GPO Access site provides access to the "List of CFR Sections Affected," described below. Once again, if the legal project that required the research drags on for several weeks or months, you should return to your sources, including administrative law sources, to make sure there were no changes during the pendency of the legal matter.

Updating print regulations does require some work. Subsequent to any CFR volume's publication, the government has continued to operate, and any given CFR provision may have been changed or withdrawn since its most recent publication. This is reflected in the Federal Register, so you will need to check the Federal Register for any changes.

To understand how CFR updating is accomplished, first examine an issue of the Federal Register. In the front, you will find a short list of "CFR Parts Affected in this Issue." That's only good for the one, daily issue. But Federal Register Publishes a separate volume (housed with the CFR's) called "**List of CFR Sections Affected**" (abbreviated "**LSA**"), a cumulative list of CFR provisions "affected" in some way in periods beginning with the last publication of the CFR volume for your section under study, and ending with the LSA issue's month. (E.g., if your section of the CFR was last published in the CFR on October 1, 1998, and you are looking at an LSA volume dated March 1999, the LSA volume will list changes from Oct. 1, 1998 to March 31, 1999.) The issue of LSA will be an "annual" accumulation of changes for the titles of the CFR published one year before the publication date of the LSA in December, March, June, and September; *e.g.,* the March issue of LSA will cumulate the year's changes for CFR titles 17-27. You must also check the latest Fed. Reg. issues following the publication date of the latest applicable LSA volume up to the date you are doing your research for the **cumulative tables of CFR Parts affected that month**.

The GPO Access web site (http://www.gpoaccess.gov) provides many of the resources needed to update federal regulations: Federal Register from 1994 to the present; CFR from 1996 to the present; LSA from 1986 to the present (note that the search or browse feature only is available from 1997 to the present). You also may use Westlaw's or Lexis's CFR databases to update regulations.

Shepard's Code of Federal Regulations Citations provides citations to specific regulations by CFR citation, and you can thereby find out if the regulation is still in force. You also can locate cases where that particular provision was at issue, as well as law review and ALR annotation references.

Chapter 5

Researching Secondary Sources of the Law: Encyclopedias, Treatises, Law Reviews, and Periodicals

By now, you probably know that secondary sources of the law, also known as secondary authorities, consist of commentary and critiques on the law written by lawyers, judges, law professors, legal scholars, and, yes, even law students. The sources vary widely in terms of breadth and depth of coverage, but it is worth grouping them together in one chapter here because *all* secondary sources have two main uses in legal research and analysis: first, as a background resource when you are not familiar with an area of law in which you are assigned to perform research and analysis, and second, as a complementary source of law used to verify your theses on the issues you are researching and to affirm your conclusions based on your specific research into the applicable jurisdiction's law.

FYI

Please do not confuse "secondary sources" with "book research." We know that some of you are convinced (wrongfully, we might add) that you will never have to research "in the books." Putting that debate aside for the moment, we cannot emphasize enough that researching secondary materials is *not the same* thing as researching "in the books." Many, if not most, secondary sources are also available on line. And so what we are talking about here is not simply about opening up printed volumes - rather, we are talking about starting your research with materials that can often put you on a surer, cleaner, clearer path to finding precisely the right primary sources that you should be looking at.

Along the same lines, secondary sources typically will not provide you with the best way to *exhaust* the law of a given jurisdiction on a specific legal issue; very few of them are focused on only one jurisdiction's law, and the vast majority of them look nationally or even internationally in their coverage of the law in an area. In addition, secondary sources generally will not be cited as a source for the applicable legal rules in your writing. (Only in rare occasions will they receive prominent billing in a rule section — primary authorities from the applicable jurisdiction must be cited in rule sections, and if such authorities exist, there rarely if ever is a need to cite a secondary authority in the rule section.) But secondary sources are very good tools for doing the two main things they are used for — background research and confirmation or justification of primary research — and thus they will be around for a long time.

I.   ENCYCLOPEDIAS

A.   Breadth of information, not depth of information

Remember this adage: a general practitioner knows nothing about everything; a specialist knows everything about nothing. Encyclopedias are general practitioners in the world of legal research. A more favorable spin on this theme is that encyclopedias are useful for their *breadth* of information, while treatises and law review articles most often are useful for their *depth* of information.

B.   When to use legal encyclopedias

Someday, you may need a brief-and-dirty introduction to an area of the law. That is all you will get in an encyclopedia, but it is necessary when you are largely unfamiliar with an area of law that you get a sense of the big picture and read about the big issues and the most basic black letter topics of the area. Encyclopedias will point you to some indicative cases; they are not the best source to find controlling cases, but they can give you an excellent head start on learning the important vocabulary on an issue, or on finding relevant authorities that will introduce you to headnotes and key numbers that can be used to expand your research (or form better electronic searches).

Encyclopedias are an official source of law, meaning that you *can* cite to them, but you should not rely exclusively on them if you can uncover primary sources that speak to your issue. That said, many judges are fond of citing them. Encyclopedias generally are reliable and well regarded for the basic, black-letter law concepts they state. But a **major treatise** that is devoted to the legal topic at hand will carry more weight in terms of persuasiveness to the extent that the same information is found in both sources. And if the concept is so basic that it shows up in an encyclopedia, it should be found in one or more controlling or potentially controlling primary authorities, which are by far the best source for the information.

C.   Main examples of encyclopedias

1.   Corpus Juris Secundum (C.J.S)

In all likelihood, you should not be surprised to find that West has attempted to corner the market in legal encyclopedias. The older West offering is Corpus Juris Secundum (C.J.S.) following up on the ever popular first edition of this set, known as Corpus Juris (the "Body of the Law").

West originally described C.J.S. as: "A complete restatement of the entire American law as developed by all reported cases." West has recently (in the last fifteen years or so) back-peddled and now calls it: "A contemporary statement of American law as derived from reported cases and legislation." More selective, less comprehensive.

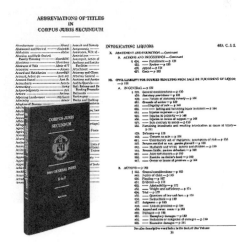

a.   How do you find information on your topic in C.J.S.?

To find information in an encyclopedia, use a words and phrases index, just like you would for a digest (West's digests refer you directly to sections of C.J.S., too), or just pull out the volume listing your topic (the volumes are arranged alphabetically by topic names) and read the section on your topic or look at the section's topical index.

b.   Can you cite to C.J.S.?

As a secondary source of law, you can cite to C.J.S., but it is definitely not a hot source, and later on you may be interrogated by your boss about why you could not find anything better. As stated above, if what you are citing is so basic that it will appear in an encyclopedia, then it should appear in some controlling primary authority. Citing primary controlling authority is by far the better practice to pursue. If you cannot find a controlling authority, cite a primary source of law as persuasive authority and consider a reference supplemental citation to C.J.S. to demonstrate that the legal principle has been adopted by multiple jurisdictions (even if not your own)). If you cannot find any (even non-controlling) persuasive case on point, then something is wrong. Look at the cases C.J.S. cites— maybe they are as old as the hills. You will have to decide then if C.J.S. still is good law and still accurate.

C.J.S. is available on Westlaw in the database "CJS."

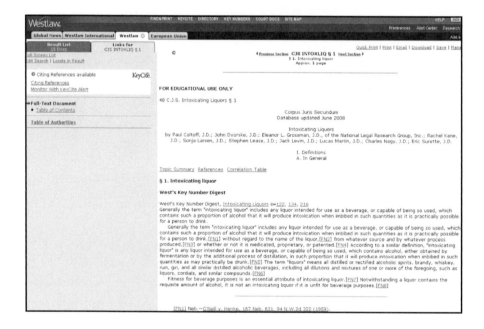

2.   American Jurisprudence Second (Am. Jur. 2d)

West's second entry in the encyclopedia market is a former Lawyer's Cooperative's product, American Jurisprudence (Am. Jur.), now in its second edition. Am. Jur. was initially the scrappy contender that challenged West's dominance, only to decide that they couldn't beat 'em, so they joined 'em.

Is Am. Jur. Better than C.J.S.? Am. Jur. is comparable to C.J.S. in many relevant particulars, such as how to find topics and volumes on your topic, but Am. Jur. overall has been regarded as a better done, more authoritative source on the law than C.J.S. Many people find it highly reliable and persuasive. Therefore, you might cite to it a little more freely than C.J.S. (but again, nothing beats a primary controlling authority that says the same thing as Am. Jur., so don't get lazy).

Am. Jur. is available on Westlaw in the AMJUR database.

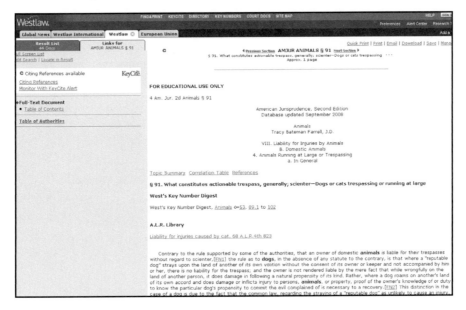

3.   Am. Jur. Proof of Facts; Am. Jur. Trials; Am. Jur. Legal Forms, and Am. Jur. Pleading and Practice Forms

American Jurisprudence has other volumes especially devoted to litigation that cover the proof of facts and trials of certain claims in certain areas of the law, and useful legal forms. Many people rave about these volumes. They are probably beyond the scope of what you have to do for this class, but definitely have a look at them if you go on to Trial Practice, Civil Practice, or a clinic.

PRACTICE POINTER

Always read the explanatory text and any introductory notes to the forms in legal form books and practice guides before you make use of them. Often these notes will tell you how to address each of the provisions of the form, and will confirm or deny that a certain form is the correct form for your client's needs.

Once again, these Am. Jur. specialty volumes are available on Westlaw in the AMJUR-POF, AMJUR-TRIALS, AMJUR-LF, and AMJUR-PP databases.

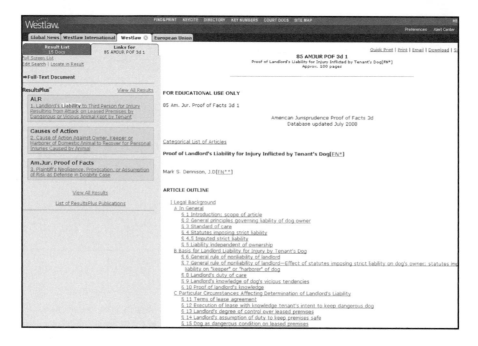

4.   State encyclopedias

State encyclopedias, such as Texas Jurisprudence or Indiana Law Encyclopedia, serve a similar function as the national encyclopedias but with a dominant or exclusive focus on the law of one state. West has published several state encyclopedias. Several of these (California, Florida, Georgia, Indiana, Maryland, Michigan, Mississippi, Ohio, and Texas) can be searched on Westlaw in whole or in various sub-topics. Virginia, West Virginia, Georgia, and Tennessee also have encyclopedias that are not published by West.

II.   TREATISES AND HORNBOOKS vs. PRACTICE GUIDES AND CLE PUBLICATIONS

Treatises come in various shapes and sizes. Some come in looseleaf binders, others come in bound volumes. Some are multi-volume, while others, especially the hornbook variety, are one volume. There are different categories of treatises, namely

1. Critical treatises;

2. Interpretive treatises;

3. Expository treatises; and

4. Student hornbooks.

The common feature of treatises is that each is painstakingly researched and drafted, and they usually are written by a legal scholar who has expertise writing in the treatise's area of study. As a result, the work of a treatise generally commands more respect among lawyers and judges, such that citation to the treatise is more welcome than citations to other secondary sources. Still, treatises are secondary authorities, but they can be very high up on the scale of persuasiveness.

Do not be confused by the quasi-treatises created by practitioners for use by other practitioners. They more particularly may be identified as:

1. Lawyers' practice guides and desktop reference books for state-specific or specialized areas of practice;

2. Continuing Legal Education (CLE)-type books from the American Law Institute and the American Bar Association (ALI-ABA), Practicing Law Institute (PLI), local bar associations, and many more.

These works might be painstakingly researched and drafted, but not always. The author might be a true expert in the area, or not—many practice guide chapters and CLE publications are ghost-written by junior associates at law firms, who then find their work published under the name of a senior partner of the firm. We've seen this happen; in fact, we've been the ghostwriters ourselves. In any event, these publications never carry the same weight as a classic treatise or hornbook. When we refer to "treatises" in the remaining portion of this chapter, we are referring to categories 1 through 4 on the preceding page, not these last two categories. We will refer to the last two categories as "practice guides" and "CLE publications."

A.   Citation to treatises—gold mine or fool's gold?

Previously, we addressed the value of treatises. In general, the name of the game is prestige, reputation, general reliability, and acceptance in the field. Some treatises are as good as gold, and you generally should feel free to cite them. Others may look like gold but you'd be panning for pyrite instead. If you are not sure about the reputation of a given treatise, ask your law professors or colleagues about the reputation of the work. You do not want to be relying heavily on a work that largely is discredited.

Hornbooks, generally speaking, have good authors and state reliable principles of black letter law. But almost every author of a hornbook will have a separate "major," multi-volume treatise on the same topic, and this specialty volume is the better authority to cite. If the language you like only is found in the hornbook, go ahead and cite it, but if it appears in both, cite the "major" treatise by the same author.

As a general rule, try not to rely on a practice guide or desk reference, especially one that is state specific and has a title like "Michigan Practice Guide" or "Nevada Civil Practice Manual." These are best left for background information, not as authority you would cite in a memo or brief. The only safe use of such authority is to add weight to an otherwise shaky citation to primary authority or to another secondary authority. Rarely should you cite one by itself for any significant legal proposition. As hinted above, some treatises look and feel like a desk reference, so you need to be sure where the work you are looking at falls. Ask your law professors and colleagues if you are wondering.

Regarding CLE publications, some of these titles can be useful, but **only** when there simply is no other legal authority on point—no cases, no digest or encyclopedia references, no law review articles, no A.L.R.s. They can be and often are the most cutting edge source on emerging areas of the law, but this is the **only** time you should think about citing them. Do not use them if the information can be found in other, "traditional" sources of the law. And be careful to use a reputable compiler of CLE materials— ALI-ABA, PLI, National Institute of Trial Advocacy ("NITA") are more reliable than state or local bar associations or other local legal associations. Finally, even if it was the only thing on earth on point, you still should hesitate to cite a CLE publication in a brief submitted to a court.

You may have noted that we did not list student help books and commercial outlines in the above lists—West's Nutshells, Gilbert's, Emmanuel's, Casenote Legal Briefs, Black Letter Law series, Shell Out the Last $25 in Your Spending Money series, Read This Instead of the Casebook series, and more titles every year. There is good reason for this:  Don't ever cite a Nutshells or Gilbert's or Emmanuel's or the ilk in any legal writing, particularly in your legal research and writing class and when you get to the actual practice of law. You would become a laughing stock of legendary proportion.

We cannot even mention in the same breath the variety of laypersons' legal guides that you may come upon—"How to do your own living will," "Do-it-yourself legal forms," "Reader's Digest Legal Guide," and computer programs such as "Willpower.™" Never think of using these for any purpose in law school or the practice of law.

B.   How do you use and update treatises?

In general, the contents of treatises may be accessed in the same way as digests or other legal sources: read the table of contents or the index, and look for other tables that orient you to the pages you think might be relevant. This is true no matter what field the treatise covers—law, psychology of child development, microbiology, stamp collecting, or other topics.

The process of updating treatises varies: some are looseleaf and readily and frequently are updated. Some get pocket parts. Some are simply not supposed to go out of style (but, like those plaid golf pants your uncle bought in 1978, tragically they do). If the treatise analyzes an area of law that changes rapidly, such as employment law or securities law, and if the work is not updated with insert pages, supplemental volumes, or pocket parts, you should be very leery of using it.

III.   RESTATEMENTS—NOT YOUR ORDINARY TREATISE

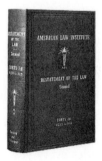

The American Law Institute ("ALI") was formed to "clean up" the law. All the best legal minds were invited to the conference. They decided to "restate" the law of certain areas in a comprehensive, highly reliable, and highly authoritative way. The aim was to create something so authoritative that even the Common Law would be brought into line—and they would be called the "Restatements of the Law." And to a large extent, this effort succeeded.

In general, restatements are *highly authoritative*—equal to the **best** treatises and almost (but not quite) equal to primary controlling authority when you use them in the explanation and application sections of your

work. If you think a primary controlling author-
ity says something contrary to a restatement, you
should have another look at the primary authority—make sure you are reading it right, and make
sure it is good law. (We said "almost" equal, because
nothing beats primary controlling authority.)

Restatements are highly reliable, largely due to the stature of the
people appointed as "reporters" of the restatements, and the peer review,
comment, revising, and redrafting procedures that the restatements un-
dergo before they are finally completed.

Note, however, that some restatements are "progressive" in nature
(some of the second and the third series of restatements especially), trying
to advocate what the law should be, rather than simply restating what it
actually is at a given moment. This is a problem, because your state may
not buy into the particular theory espoused in the particular restatement
section you are examining. Be careful. Just because you find an answer
to a legal question in a restatement does not mean you are finished. You
must check to make sure your jurisdiction follows this provision of the
restatement, and if it does, whether it has modified, explained, limited,
expanded, or done something else with it. You must always answer the
question, how does this section of the restatement work in this state?

IV.   UNIFORM LAWS

Uniform Laws are a model for legislation—a
statutory regime on a topic—that are drafted so that
each state can have a chance to adopt the same form of
statute on this topic. Uniform laws are drafted and re-
drafted, commented on and criticized by legal scholars,
so that they are highly tuned and authoritative models
for passage in all 50 states. Major examples are The
Uniform Commercial Code, the Uniform Fraudulent
Transfer Act, and the Model Penal Code.

Because of their "uniform" nature, the interpretation of a provision of a uniform law by one state is more often than not held to be very

persuasive in other states. This factor is an added boost to the persuasive authority of a court in a sister state.

V.   LAW REVIEWS, LAW JOURNALS

A.   A complicated topic

You rarely will appreciate how complex, how troublesome, how many issues (old, present, and emerging issues) are involved, and simply what is at stake in an area of law until you read a law review article on that subject. Reading (and writing) law review articles of- ten is a humbling experience. A good law review article takes months to research and write. The authors of law review articles—law professors, practitioners, judges, and law students—strive to plumb the depths of an area of law and present a detailed exposition of the old and new problems, issues, and simply stated, what is going on in an area. There is a drive to print articles on current and emerging topics; you will not find too many recent articles on negligence of railroad operators, unless there recently was some new development in the law of this area.

B.   More than you can shake a stick at?

Over the last seventy years, the law review and law journal printing business has boomed. It used to be one journal per school—The Harvard Law Review, The Yale Law Journal, The Washington University Law Quarterly. Then things got topical, more focused, and so now there is the Columbia Journal of Transnational Law, Richmond Journal of Law and Technology, Iowa State Hog Farming Law Review (planned for 2010). At last count, Harvard and Georgetown had ten journals each.

C.   The table of contents is easy to find

The table of contents of individual copies of a law review is printed on the cover of the booklet. As indicated by these tables of contents, the featured works found in law reviews and law journals fall into several categories:

1. Articles—the full-blown exposition on an area of law with topical current events interest. Written most often by a law professor, but sometimes by a practitioner, judge, or other expert.

2. Notes—student articles, similar to the above. Sometimes referring to a student article about a recent case, rule, or statute and what it does to the law in a given area.

3. Comments—written by students, law professors or practitioners, they are less than a full article, and often comment on a recently controversial, disputed area of the law. Sometimes they refer to a short article about a recent change (case, rule, statute) in the law, so the definition intersects with Notes above.

4. Commentary (Essays, Correspondence)—talking heads compete, saying "this is what the law should be," and pick apart each others' opinions.

5. Symposium issue—an issue devoted to one theme or devoted to reprinting of the speeches and presentations of a major conference at the law school.

D.　Are you supposed to be impressed?

Yes, law review articles can be truly impressive, full of information, incredibly well researched, and stunning in their conclusions, but . . . the big question: **should you cite to them?**

Law reviews, in general, are high on the list of persuasive secondary authorities. Of course, as secondary authorities, no law review article will substitute for primary legal authority, and certainly not for primary controlling legal authority. The persuasive value of a given article depends on several factors. Perhaps first and foremost on the author—famous names in the law get attention and respect. The best author is a nationally known and recognized figure in the area of law in which the article is

written. If a famous mind steps out of their area of expertise to write—
Professor John Coffee leaves securities and mergers and acquisitions law
and decides to do a piece on Irish criminal law— the article still is valuable, but not as amazing as the situation where the expert writes on a topic
within her expertise.

The value also (but not always) may depend on the law review or
law journal itself. That said, the most prestigious scholars often publish
outside of their institutions, and these articles garner attention and respect
regardless. As with all secondary authorities, however, if garbage went
in, garbage will come out. It matters a great deal if an individual article
is well researched, well reasoned, well written, and simply that it makes
sense. Even Arthur Miller makes mistakes, and some of them even get
published.

E.   Compared to other secondary authorities, where do law review articles rank?

Subject to the criteria above, law reviews generally are much better
authority than an A.L.R. But they are not necessarily better than a treatise.
Major, multi-volume treatises (like Wright & Miller, <u>Federal Practice and
Procedure</u>) carry more weight, mainly because these important treatises
must stand the test of time before they become accepted and admired.
So an old way of thinking that stands up for years can tip the scales more
than a fresh perspective on a hot topic. Of course, a good law review article is better than a mediocre treatise.

In addition, law reviews generally are better than encyclopedias in
terms of persuasive authority. But they are, of course, used for a different
purpose than encyclopedias. Specifically, you will not use a law review article primarily for finding cases, although this can be an incidental benefit
of a well-researched article.

F.   Finding law review articles

If you are trying to locate law review articles by hand (*i.e.*, without using a computer), the first place to look is the current Index of Legal
Periodicals. It is organized like most indices we have been mentioning in
this book. Your law school reference librarian can help you out with this
resource the first time you go on a search.

Far simpler and quicker than these print indices are the law review databases available on-line on Westlaw, Lexis, and the Internet. Westlaw and Lexis each let you search for articles by word or phrase or topic or author. You can search the entire database or more focused databases defined by type of publication, subject matter, geography, or date, or a combination of these factors.

VI.   OTHER PERIODICALS

Just as practice guides and desk reference works can masquerade as a treatise, bar journals and legal magazines can be similar to law reviews in appearance, but as a rule, they are not as detailed, comprehensive, or authoritative as a law review. They contain nuts and bolts, practice-oriented material. Thus, they only are as authoritative as the average practice guide or CLE publication. Rank these lower than treatises and A.L.R.s.

Legal newspapers, newsletters, and special interest publications—on topics such as international law, elder law, law and economics—once again rarely are as detailed, comprehensive, or authoritative as a law review. Thus, they are not as authoritative as true law review articles. Use them as you would a CLE publication, unless you notice that the author of the work is a superstar.

Chapter 6

Researching Legislative History

I.   WHAT IS LEGISLATIVE HISTORY?

Legislative history is a term used to designate the documents and materials that contain the historical and background information generated while a bill or other legislative action is on its way to becoming a law. It includes draft versions of the bill, redrafts, testimony at various hearings on the bill, committee reports, studies, legislative floor debates, executive messages, and other materials generated in this process.

PRACTICE POINTER

Is legislative history admissible in all cases?
It is a matter of active debate in the United States whether evidence of legislative history should be "admissible" in all cases, no cases, or only where a showing of ambiguity in the relevant, operative terms of the statute or rule is established. Its persuasive value thus is interpreted differently by different courts and other arbiters. This chapter does not take up or continue the debate. Simply be warned that the existence of legislative history and the ability to research it effectively does not guaranty that you will be able to use it to support an interpretation of a statute or rule.

II. FOR WHAT PURPOSES IS LEGISLATIVE HISTORY USED?

One use of legislative history is simply to monitor the progress of a bill or other action to determine its status (prior to enactment into law). But it also may be used in some circumstances as a source of persuasive authority, specifically to determine "legislative intent"— what the legislature meant when it wrote or rewrote the text of a bill (and eventually the law) a certain way. This evidence may be used to further argue an interpretation of the law or to attempt to resolve ambiguities created by the words of a statute. As noted above in the Practicale Pointer, however, different courts (and judges) have different views concerning the value that should be assigned to legislative history, which often depend on the circumstances in which the history is invoked (and the precise kind of history at issue). Some judges devalue legislative history because you typically can find evidence to support basically *any point* you want to make. This is especially true if the legislative history for a given statute is extensive. That said, there certainly is considerable merit in knowing how to research legislative history even if it ultimately proves useful only as background information or context of the law.

In contrast, the theory behind the usefulness of legislative history is that each progressive addition, deletion, and alteration in the language of a bill is direct evidence of deliberate thinking on the part of the legislators who contributed to the creation of the law. For example:

> If a bill originally stated that dog-owners were to be excluded from its coverage, but this exclusion was written out of the bill just prior to enactment into law, one could argue persuasively that the legislature intended to include dog-owners within the coverage of the statute.

> If a legal standard in the law was originally phrased as "actual knowledge," and the bill was later amended in this section to state a standard of "actual or constructive knowledge," one could argue that the legislature intended the standard of knowledge to be lower than and certainly not the same as "actual knowledge."

The reports generated by committees and conferences, and the floor debates where questions about the statute and explanations of the meaning of the terms are discussed, are also taken to be evidence of legislative intent. For example:

> If the sponsor of a bill told the House of Representatives in a speech on the floor of the House that the law would definitely encompass dog-owners in its scope, and nothing else in the debate contradicts this statement, one could argue that the representatives understood the law to cover dog-owners when they voted on the law.

III.   LEGISLATIVE HISTORY AS LEGAL AUTHORITY

Legislative history is *not* a source of the law and it is never to be considered primary controlling authority. The terms of the statute itself are the only primary, potentially controlling legal authority regarding the law created by the statute. However, legislative history is not simply commentary. It is not simply a secondary persuasive authority, such as a treatise or law review, that discusses the meaning of a statute. It is evidence of legislative intent (or at least of the intent of individual legislators) prior to the fact of enactment that goes beyond the realm of interpretations by third-parties after the fact. Thus, in many instances, it will carry more persuasive weight than even the commentary and interpretation of a great legal scholar.

Because the goal of statutory interpretation always is to determine the meaning of the statutory text, evidence of the authors' understanding of that text is relevant and helpful to finding the meaning of difficult or ambiguous terms. In a situation where one particular piece of legislative history directly answers a question or resolves an ambiguity in the absence of other pieces of legislative history that produce contrary inferences, then the use of such uncontroverted history to discern the meaning of the text is prudent and appropriate.

As we have already noted, however, there is a basic and undeniable tension created by attempts to use legislative history in litigation or other legal fora. There is a long-standing and strongly supported school of thought that statutes should be interpreted on the basis of the terms of the statutory text alone. Though certain rules or "canons" of statutory construction (especially those concerning how language is read) may aid the process of reading and applying the text, but it is the text that should govern the meaning of the statute. Stated otherwise, many jurists maintain that ambiguities in statutory language are to be resolved textually (the logical meaning of the terms used in the statute) and contextually (the logical meaning of the statute as a whole and its meaning in the context of the existing law on the topic), but not by resorting to evidence of the drafters' intent.

But as an advocate, you may not always be pleased with the way the terms of a statute are likely to be read and applied if your client is on the short end of that equation. So, it is common practice for advocates to search for support for a beneficial interpretation amidst the legislative history. Courts may be especially likely to pay attention to legislative history where it bolsters an argument or a reading premised on other authority (and not on the drafters' alleged intent alone). The bottom line is that advocates will keep digging for it and thrusting it under the courts' noses, and the courts will keep reading it and writing opinions that adopt arguments for interpretation that rely on legislative history. So, the study of legislative history is here to stay.

IV.   WHAT DOCUMENTS AND MATERIALS MAKE UP LEGISLATIVE HISTORY?

FYI

For a review of the legislative process on Westlaw, you might consider consulting the following powerpoint: http://lawschool.westlaw.com/research/InstructionalAids.asp?SecondaryPage=3.

Legislative history generally consists of two components: the first is the chronology of events for the legislation in question—whether and when the bill was introduced, referred to committee or subcommittee, reported out, debated, sent to conference, voted on, and signed into law. The second component is the documents and testimony that were produced during the course of the chronology. To investigate and analyze these two components intelligently, it is necessary to understand the process by which legislation is enacted. (See <u>Chapter 2</u>, above).

The cornerstone necessary for researching legislative history for a particular law is the bill number and the subsequent Public Law number. Bills are numbered sequentially in the order they are introduced. If they fail to be enacted in a given Congress, but are reintroduced in a subsequent Congress, their number will change with each new Congress. As a bill progresses through the legislative process, it may generate several different kinds of documents. Not every bill generates the same number and type of legislative history documents—it all depends on how complicated or troublesome the legislation was or how it was handled by the two chambers prior to enactment.

After a bill is introduced and numbered, it is assigned to a committee. Committees produce four different types of documents: Committee Prints, Committee Documents, Hearings, and Reports.

Committee Prints are compiled by the administrative staff of a Congressional committee as background for the committee members. They contain statistical data and background information and may be reproduced from such sources as the Congressional Research Service.

Committee Documents are sent to the committee by administrative agencies or the executive branch. Generally, they contain facts and information regarding the subject matter of the bill.

Hearings come in two forms: legislative committee hearings to receive testimony in support of (or against) bills currently before the House of Representatives or Senate, and investigative hearings on important issues which are not the subject of pending legislation, but which may lead to legislation in the future.

Committee Reports are written by the members of the committee and contain recommendations on why the bill should be passed. The report usually contains the text of the bill, an analysis of its content and meaning, and the committee's rationale for its recommendations. There may also be a minority statement if there was a disagreement among the committee members. Of all the documents to come out of committee, the Committee Report generally is considered to be the most important in establishing legislative intent, because it contains the legislators' own words and contemporaneous construction of the meaning of the legislation and it is intended to guide the thinking of the entire legislature on the meaning of the legislation.

At this point, the reported bill is sent back to the appropriate chamber for consideration. Floor debates along with amendments and votes on the legislation are contained in the **Congressional Record**.

Floor debates are considered to be another source of direct evidence of legislative intent, again because they are the legislators' own words. However, please note that the actual record of any given debate may be called into question because each Congressman can amend and edit the record of their remarks on the floor before the final version is recorded in the Congressional Record, and she even can submit prepared remarks and statements into the Record that were never actually delivered to the members of the chamber, and no one knows whether any legislator other than the author knew anything about the remarks. (Since March 1978, such inserted remarks are preceded and closed in the Congressional Record by a bullet (•), so that the researcher can know the material was not actually delivered to the chamber.)

If a conference is required to reconcile different versions of a bill that were debated and approved in the Senate and the House, a conference report may be generated. Note: no transcript or record of the proceedings of the conference committee is made, so the report generally is all you have to go on.

Conference Reports, even more than Committee Reports, are held to be important in establishing legislative intent, because they contain a contemporaneous construction and explanation of the meaning of the legislation from representatives of both chambers prior to the final consideration of the legislation by the two chambers. The conference report will appear in one of the following formats: (a) In two parts consisting of the text of the agreed language of the bill and a discussion known as the "Joint Explanation of the Conferees;" or (b) Only the text of the sections where compromise was needed.

Researchers also should be aware of the following facts regarding Conference Reports:

1. After the conference report is officially filed it goes to the House and Senate for debate. Technically, once on the floor it cannot be amended. However, legislators occasionally are able to manipulate the rules to their favor and make amendments.

2. The conference report always is printed in the Congressional Record in the House section.

3. Usually, researchers will be able to obtain a copy of a conference report from the House or Senate Document Room. However, if the conference report has generated a lot of interest (such as the Tax Reform Act of 1986) it will be sold by

the GPO.

4. Specialized commercial services such as CCH or Prentice-Hall will reprint conference reports relevant to their subject matter in their various loose-leaf volumes on the topic of the statute.

5. The conference report will be cited as "H. Rept.", not as "H. Conf. Rept." If the Senate requested a printing of conference report it will be cited as "S. Rept." One may also see a citation to both a House and Senate conference reports. Such reports are identical and only one version need be obtained.

After each chamber of Congress has agreed upon the final version of a bill, the enrolled bill is sent to the President for signature, and if signed, it becomes a law and is published as a Slip Law.

Consider the following graphical depiction of the process:

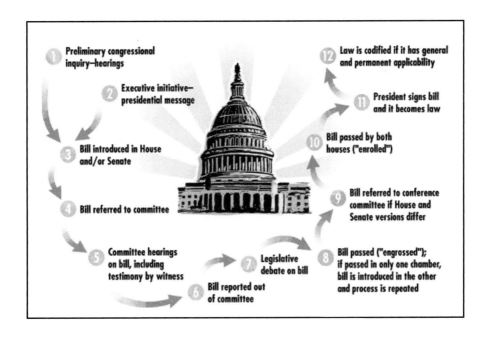

V.   HOW TO COMPILE A LEGISLATIVE HISTORY USING WESTLAW OR LEXIS

It has become a great deal easier to compile the legislative history for federal legislation now that Westlaw and Lexis have made a special effort to link you into these documents and research materials. If you have a fee-paying client who is willing to foot the bill for fee-based on-line research, this should be your first option.

A.   Compiled legislative histories on Westlaw and Lexis

There are some legislative histories of major pieces of federal legislation that already have been compiled and made available to you on Westlaw. Using a compiled legislative history is one of the best time-saving devices you ever will encounter in your legal career.

Arnold and Porter's Compiled Legislative Histories for Selected Laws on Westlaw contains the compiled legislative histories of a dozen or more major pieces of legislation, including several important civil rights and discrimination laws from the 1960's and 70's. These were compiled by the Arnold and Porter law firm.

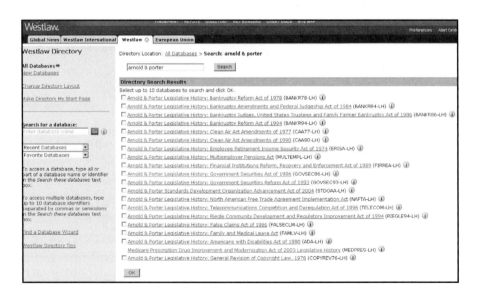

Lexis has compiled histories collected by CIS (Congressional Information Service):

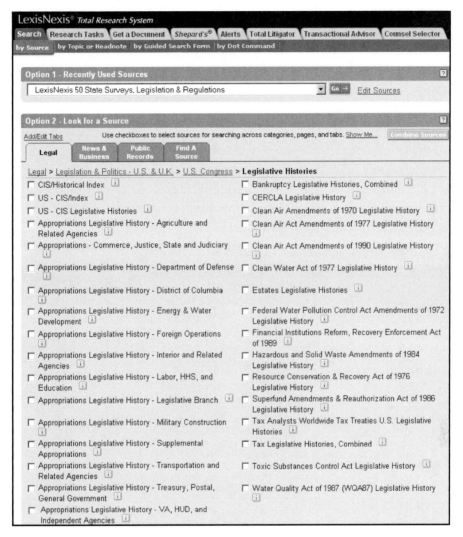

When a compiled history is not available, you must then take the next step which is to compile your own legislative history. Once again, the fee-based on-line services are ready to help you.

B.   Compiling your own legislative history on Westlaw or Lexis

The fee-based services have made legislative history one more part of the package of research tools they deliver with the statutes and bills (pending legislation) sources they offer in their legislation databases. All federal and many of the states' legislation is tracked, and federal committee reports, records of amendments, and floor debates from the Congressional Record are available to you in each service's legislation databases. The coverage does not go back in time forever, but it should be useful for collecting legislative history documents for legislation enacted within the last fifteen to twenty years.

If you are looking at a statutory section on one of the services, you can move from that screen directly to legislative history sources linked to the statute's page. The process is very similar on both Westlaw and Lexis. We will demonstrate the technique using Westlaw and investigate the legislative history of the Digital Millennium Copyright Act provisions preventing you from circumventing or decrypting an electronic protection of copyrighted material, for instance on DVDs or encrypted databases.

After you pull up the statutory section (17 U.S.C. § 1201), you have two entry points to the legislative history. One is the KeyCite links:

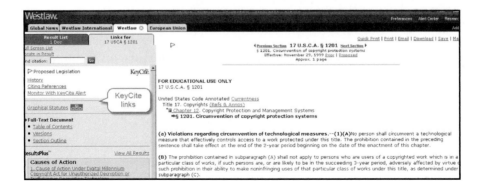

The other is the Legislative History links lower down in the left column:

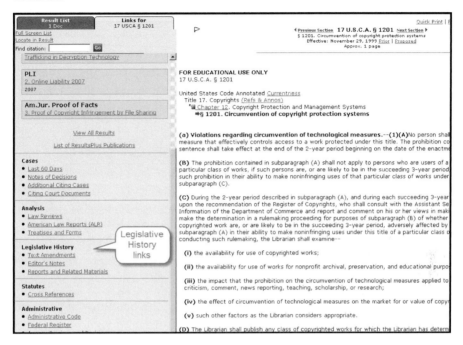

The Graphical Statutes link in the KeyCite section will produce a diagram showing the available legislative history documents (including "future history" in the form of proposed amendments to the statute):

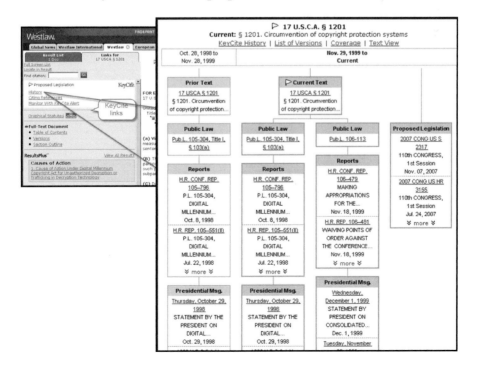

From there, you can click on the links to bring up specific documents, such as H.R. Conf. Rep. 105-796:

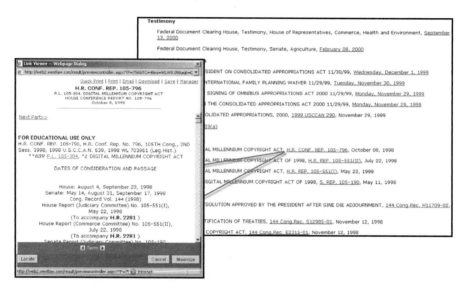

Clicking on the History link in the KeyCite Section will produce the same legislative history information in list form, and you can click on the linked documents in the list:

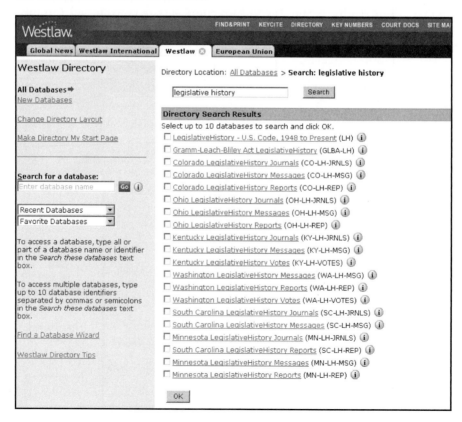

The same list shown directly above will be summoned if you click the "Reports and Related Materials" link in the Legislative History section of the left column of the main screen for the statutory section.

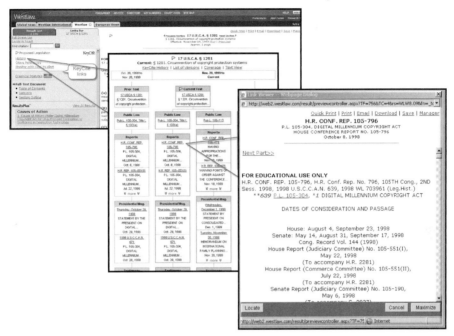

The process above works for federal legislation *introduced after 1990.* For legislation introduced from 1948 to 1989, the availability of committee reports on Westlaw is limited to those reported in U.S. Code, Congressional, and Administrative News (USCCAN), and USCCAN only printed reports on select, high-profile legislation. Westlaw carries presidential signing statements from 1986 forward, and reports the debates on federal legislation in the Congressional Record (CR database) from 1985 forward.

With state legislation, the research process is the same for those states that publish legislative history, but not all of them do. You can check with a reference librarian at a law library in the state (or at a law school located in the state) to find out whether the state legislature generates reports and other documents or even records the debates of the state legislature. If the state does, it will be accessible through the same type of KeyCite links (History or Graphical Statutes) or Legislative History link (Reports and Related Materials).

There are additional Westlaw databases for legislative history information for state legislation:

One auspiciously named database on Westlaw is the **LH** database that purports to be "Legislative History of the U.S. Code from 1948 to the present." What this database actually contains is the record of USCCAN committee reports on selected federal legislation from 1948 to 1989, a full history of all committee reports on federal legislation from 1990 to the present, and presidential signing statements from 1986 forward.

VI.   HOW TO COMPILE A LEGISLATIVE HISTORY USING ON-LINE SOURCES

A.   Thomas - the Library of Congress legislative website

An excellent free resource for researching federal legislative history is the "Thomas" Library of Congress website (www.thomas.gov). Thomas collects many of the legislative history materials for fairly recent federal legislation (passed since 1995)[1], but its coverage could theoretically expand in the future.

---

1 Thomas's coverage includes: House and Senate Committee Reports (1995 – present); Bills (1989–present); Public Laws by public law number (1973–present); Bill Summary & Status (1973–present); Congressional Record (1989–present); Index to the Congressional Record (1995–present).

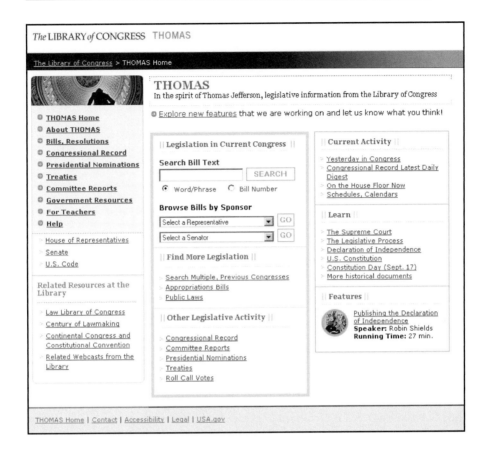

B.   State legislative history sites

Researching the legislative history of state statutes can be considerably more challenging than researching federal legislative history, though advances in state-sponsored websites is making the process easier all the time. As mentioned above, some state legislatures operate like Congress and print and record legislative history committee reports and debates for bills and laws that pass through the legislature. Others do not. If, after consulting a good reference librarian in a law library in the state, you find out that the state has legislative history, you can follow that person's suggestions on how to find it, or look for one of the state legislature's sites discussed in Chapter 2 above, e.g., http://www.assembly.ca.gov/clerk/BILLSLEGISLATURE/BILLSLEGISLATURE.HTM

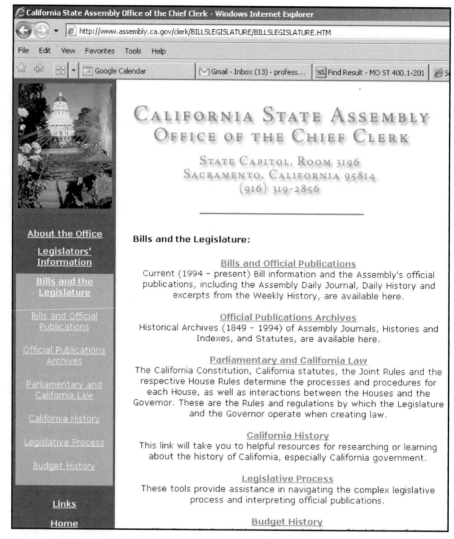

You also can start with the law library of the Indiana University School of Law—Bloomington which has compiled a list of on-line resources for state legislative history: http://www.law.indiana.edu/lawlibrary/research/guides/statelegislative/index.shtml.

Another source would be the Multistate Associates Inc.'s "State Legislative Presence on the Internet" site, http://www.multistate.com/site.nsf/state?OpenPage.

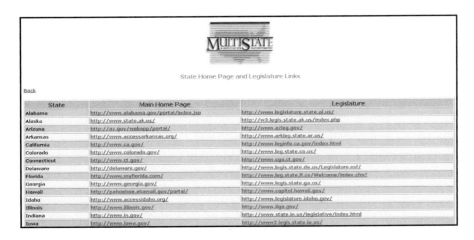

VII.   HOW TO COMPILE A FEDERAL LEGISLATIVE HISTO-RY USING PRINT RESOURCES

To research the legislative history of a federal statute using print resources, you need to know at least one of the following things before you can start your legislative history:

Bill number and date introduced; or

Public Law number and date enacted.

You can find these numbers and names in several places including:

1. "Bill Tracking Reports" available on Westlaw or Lexis in the resource areas for federal or state legislation.

2. CIS Legislative History volumes, index of subjects and names.

3. CCH Congressional Index. The "Enactments" section gives bill number for public laws and public law numbers for bills.

4. Statutes at Large and the U.S. Code Congressional & Administrative News (U.S.C.C.A.N.) are arranged by public law number, and list bill number and short title for each public law. The United States Code Service also issues monthly pamphlets with new public laws.

5. Congressional Record Index. The subject index gives bill numbers, and the "History of Bills and Resolutions", arranged by bill number, gives public law numbers for enacted bills. The table of "History of Bills Enacted into Public Law" in the Daily Digest, arranged by public law number, gives bill numbers for each public law. Beginning with 1985, the Congressional Record and Daily Digest can also be searched on Lexis and Westlaw.

6. United States Code Annotated (U.S.C.A.) and United States

Code Service (U.S.C.S.). The public law number and date of enactment are given in "history notes" following each U.S. Code section.

7. If you know the name of the act, the "Popular Name Table" in the U.S.C., U.S.C.S., and U.S.C.A. will give you the public law number. Shepard's Acts and Cases by Popular Name gives the public law number and date enacted.

8. The Congressional Quarterly Weekly Report (CQ) has a weekly status table of major legislation. It is particularly good for tracking complex legislation such as appropriations bills. The annual Congressional Quarterly Almanac (Law Reference) gives a summary legislative history for public laws.

A.   Compiled legislative histories in print

Once you have the name of an act and the public law number, check the library catalog (or a reference librarian) to find out if your law library has a compiled legislative history for your law. The two most widely used bibliographies of compiled legislative histories in print media are:

Nancy P. Johnson, <u>Sources of Compiled Legislative Histories</u> (2000)

Bernard Reams, <u>Federal Legislative Histories: An Annotated Bibliography and Index to Officially Published Sources</u> (1994)

B.   Legislative history of a federal bill – 1970 to the present

If your library does not have a published history, use the guidelines below to compile your own. The set of steps outlined here is only one of several methods of compiling a legislative history.

• Congressional Information Service's CIS Index and CIS Abstracts and the annual CIS Legislative History volumes.

There is a CIS Index for the U.S. Serial Set (committee reports), U.S. Congressional Committee Hearings, and U.S. Congressional Committee Prints (covering the years 1833 to 1969). The <u>Congressional Information Service</u>'s Digest of Public General Bills and Resolutions began in 1936 and allows you to trace a bill from the public law number. The Monthly Catalog goes back to 1896 and covers documents published by the United States printing office.

<u>Congressional Information Service</u>'s Legislative History volumes provide the following:

A. Beginning with 1984, the Legislative History volume contains histories of every public law: complete citations, with abstracts, of every public law, plus related hearings, reports, committee prints, bills, debates, plus bibliographic references, without citations, to related bills.

B. From 1970 to 1983, the Legislative History section appeared in the back of the annual <u>Abstracts</u> volume and contained only citations to documents, with references to the abstracts elsewhere in the volume.

C. CIS gives only the dates of debates. To find the page number of debates in the Congressional Record, use the Congressional Record Index. The "History of Bills and Resolutions" in the annual index volume lists all the pages where a bill is mentioned or debated. (For sessions of Congress after 1981, there is not yet an annual Congressional Record Index; rather, there are only biweekly indexes. Each index gives the complete history of bills acted upon during the two weeks covered.)

C.   Legislative history of a federal bill introduced before 1970

1.   To find committee reports and documents:

Use the CIS U.S. Serial Set Index. The subject/key word index gives complete titles of reports and documents, lists the type of report (Senate report, House report, etc.), Congress, session and the Serial Set volume number where reports are bound. There is a complete numerical listing and schedule of Serial Set volumes that is more comprehensive than the Government Printing Office's own Numerical Lists. For the years 1893-1940, you can also use the Document Catalog. Each volume is a catalog of government publications issued during one Congress. Entries are listed under subject, personal author, issuing agency or committee, and sometimes title. Complete bibliographical information, including serial set volume numbers, is provided for Reports and Documents. The Document Catalog is still useful, but it is less inclusive than the various CIS indexes, with respect to Congressional documents.

2. To find committee hearings:

Use the CIS US Congressional Committee Hearings Index. This set also is published by the Congressional Information Service, and it provides complete citations and brief abstracts for hearings from 1833 to 1969. The Senate Library Index of Congressional Committee Hearings & Supplements and Shelf-list of Congressional Committee Hearings is useful for looking up hearings before 1979, but in general, both should be considered superseded by the CIS indices. Alternatively, you may try to find the information in the Document Catalog and the Monthly Catalog. There is also the CIS Unpublished Senate Committee Hearings Index. The index currently covers 1823 through 1964, but the material will be supplemented. Copies of these hearings are available on microfiche from CIS.

3. To find committee prints:

The best source is the CIS US Congressional Committee Prints Index. This companion to the Hearings Index also provides a detailed subject and name index, and a brief abstract of each print. You also can use the Monthly Catalog and the Documents Catalog to identify earlier prints.

4. To find floor debates:

If you are on-line, search the Congressional Record on Westlaw or Lexis. If you are limited to books, use the Congressional Record Index. The "History of Bills and Resolutions" in the annual index volume lists all the pages where a bill is mentioned or debated.

VIII.   HOW TO COMPILE A STATE LEGISLATIVE HISTORY USING PRINT RESOURCES

As mentioned above, when approaching the task of compiling a legislative history of a state statute, the best practice is to visit a law library in the state (or view the law library's web page) or to call a reference librarian at a major law school in the state or at the state's legislature or court of last resort. It also is possible to go to the state legislature's web site or the state bar association's website and see if the information is present on the Internet.

Not every state collects and retains legislative history. In some states, there is no record of legislation other than a record of the bills introduced and amendments made to the bills prior to the bills' passage. In other states, audio recordings of floor debates or committee proceedings are made and retained, but access to the recordings and the ability to make copies of the recordings is not guaranteed in each of these states. Therefore, an inquiry to a knowledgeable law librarian in the state is the first and best step to finding out whether and how to perform research into the legislative history of the state's laws.

Chapter 7

Researching Court Rules, Local Rules, and Subject-Specific Resources

I.   COURT RULES

This section examines the federal rules of procedure and evidence that apply in federal court.

A.   Federal rules of "general" application

The following rules are of general application in the federal courts:

Federal Rules of Civil Procedure (cited as Fed. R. Civ. P., first promulgated in 1938): These rules instruct litigants in how to proceed in civil cases in federal court. The rules cover timing issues, content and construction of pleadings, parties and joinder issues, discovery standards and methods of discovery, trials, post-trial motions, judgments, and other issues of procedure. The official version of the rules is found in the Appendix to Title 28 of the U.S. Code.

Federal Rules of Criminal Procedure (cited as Fed. R. Crim. P., first promulgated in 1946): These rules instruct litigants in how to conduct a criminal case in federal court. The official version of the rules is found in the Appendix to Title 18 of the U.S. Code, along with the Federal Sentencing Guidelines and the Rules for Conducting Trial of Misdemeanors before U.S. Magistrate Judges.

Federal Rules of Appellate Procedure (cited as Fed. R. App. P., first promulgated in 1968): These rules instruct litigants in how to conduct an appeal in federal appellate courts. The official version of the rules is found in the Appendix to Title 28 of the U.S. Code.

Federal Rules of Evidence (cited as Fed. R. Evid., first promulgated in 1975): These are the rules regarding the relevance, admissibility, foundation and capacity, and requirements of evidence and witnesses in civil and criminal trials in federal court. The official version of the rules is found in the Appendix to Title 28 of the U.S. Code.

B.   Sources regarding the federal rules of general application

Appendix to Title 28 of the United States Code—As mentioned above, the unannotated, official versions of the Federal Rules of Civil Procedure, the Federal Rules of Appellate Procedure, and the Federal Rules of Evidence are printed in the Appendix to Title 28 of the United States Code. Also included are the Judicial Conference Advisory Committee Notes ("Advisory Committee Notes"), which are contemporaneous constructions and explanations of the rules by the general committee responsible for recommending changes and additions to the rules.

U.S.C.A., U.S.C.S.—Annotated versions of the rules and Advisory Committee Notes are found in the United States Code Annotated (West) and the United States Code Service (West, formerly Lawyers Coop). As with the code itself, U.S.C.A. promises that its annotations contain comprehensive coverage of all cases citing a rule or rules, while U.S.C.S. promises selective, theoretically more relevant annotations to cases that actually say something important about a rule or rules. The **U.S.C.A.** also prints "Practice Commentaries" on certain rules; <u>e.g.</u>, Fed. R. Civ. P. 45. These notes are useful to the practitioner, but are not as persuasive as the Advisory Committee Notes when used as an interpretative authority.

Federal Procedure, Lawyers Edition (West, formerly Lawyers Coop)—Contains all the federal rules of general application and the Advisory Committee Notes on the rules. Other volumes include the local rules for all the circuit courts of appeals, and the local rules for all the district courts in the country.

Federal Rules Service (West, formerly Lawyers Coop)—Collects and prints the federal rules of general application, and publishes cases interpreting the federal rules, including cases that are otherwise unpublished in the Federal Reporter, Federal Supplement, or Federal Rules Decisions (but are generally found on Westlaw and Lexis). Parts of the series include the **Federal Rules Service reporter** (for the cases), **Federal Rules Digest** (classifying the cases reported in digest form), **Federal Court Local Rules**, and **Finding Aids volumes** (which are considered useful in locating the information you need from the other volumes in the set).

Federal Rules of Evidence Series (West, formerly Lawyers Coop)—Similar to the Federal Rules Service, it publishes cases interpreting the Federal Rules of Evidence, including cases that are otherwise unpublished in the Federal Reporter, Federal Supplement, or Federal Rules Decisions (but are generally found on Westlaw and Lexis). It also has a **Reporter** series, **Digest**, and **Finding Aids volumes** devoted to the Federal Rules of Evidence.

Federal Rules Decisions (F.R.D.) (West)—A reporter series that publishes federal cases that interpret the federal rules of general application. Cases reported in these volumes are not reported in Federal Supplement or Federal Reporter. They also print updates and amendments to the rules, and some drafting "legislative" history, judiciary committee and Federal Judicial Center reports, and general commentary on the rules.

West's Rules Pamphlets—West yearly puts out very useful pamphlets of the major federal rules of general application for civil cases and criminal cases. The civil volume is called **Federal Civil Judicial Procedure and Rules**, and it contains the Federal Rules of Civil Procedure, Appellate Procedure, and Evidence, Rules of the Judicial Panel on Multi-District Litigation, Rules of the U.S. Supreme Court, the U.S. Constitution, and portions of the text of Title 28 of the U.S. Code. The criminal volume is called **Federal Criminal Code and Rules**, and it contains the Federal Rules of Criminal Procedure, Appellate Procedure, and Evidence, the

Rules of the U.S. Supreme Court, the complete text of Title 18 of the U.S. Code, which lays out most federal crimes, and portions of Titles 15, 21, 26, 28, 31, 41, and 46 of the U.S. Code that contain other federal criminal laws.

West has an interesting way of updating its rules pamphlets—if a yearly pamphlet goes out of date during the year (unexpectedly or not), West will "quickly" issue a little paste-in pocket part and try to get it out to all of its customers who bought the yearly pamphlet. Various reasons that might cause this to happen are that a large number of new rules are promulgated, or several old rules are significantly amended, or some other important development occurs. Routine or minor changes to a few rules or the addition of only a small number of rules will not prompt this kind of treatment.

Westlaw and Lexis—the full text of the rules of general application and the Advisory Committee Notes, and even some drafting "legislative" history, are found on-line. For example, on Westlaw, you can search the following databases:

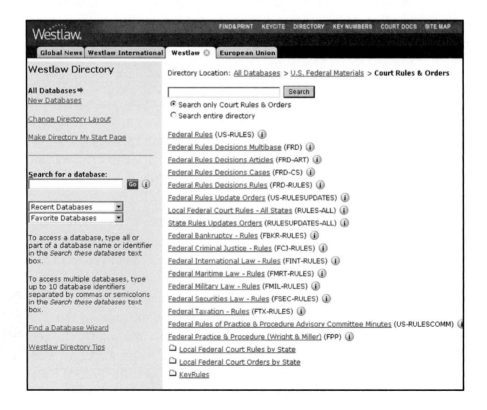

US-RULES—Federal Rules of general application are found in the US-RULES database. It contains the text of all the rules, Advisory Committee Notes, and Practice Commentaries. These databases are taken from the U.S.C.A., so they are automatically annotated. You can limit your search using the citation (ci) field; e.g., if you only want rules from the Fed. R. Civ. P., you can put "ci(frcp)" in your search.

US-RULESUPDATES—Federal Rules Update Orders are found in the US-RULESUPDATES database. The database contains the amendments and additions to the rules in the "Rules" databases occurring between publication of the official text of the rules. The amendments are often promulgated by an administrative order of a court (e.g., the U.S. Supreme Court), hence the name for the database. The database also contains commentary and reports issued by the Judicial Conference Advisory Committee and its Standing Committees on the Rules, or from the Federal Judicial Center, that pertain to certain rules.

RULES-ALL—Local Federal Court Rules for all states are found in the RULES-ALL database.

xx-RULES—Local Federal Court Rules and state court rules for a particular state are identified by state abbreviation xx-RULES; e.g., MO-RULES. The database will include all districts within the state; e.g., MO-RULES contains the rules for the Western District of Missouri and the Eastern District of Missouri and any local rules for federal bankruptcy and tax courts in those districts. This database also includes all the rules of procedure for state courts, e.g., MO-RULES contains the Missouri Supreme Court Rules, and the local rules for the individual state courts, such as the Local Rules for the Missouri Circuit Court, 22nd Judicial Circuit, St. Louis City. Again, they are based on West's products for the state, so they automatically are annotated.

RULESUPDATES-ALL—Local Federal Court Orders for all States are found in the RULESUPDATES-ALL database. It is an "orders" database, as described above.

xx-RULESUPDATES—Local Federal Court Orders by State are in the xx-RULESUPDATES database; e.g., IL-RULESUP-DATES

FBKR-RULES—a database containing the Federal Bankruptcy Rules from Title 11 of the U.S. Code.

FCJ-RULES—Federal Criminal Justice rules are found in the FCJ-RULES database. These include the Federal Rules of Criminal Procedure; the Rules for Misdemeanor Trials before U.S. Magistrates; and Habeas Corpus rules for actions under 28 U.S.C. §§ 2854 and 2855.

FINT-RULES—Federal International Law Rules for the Court of International Trade and other international proceedings.

FMRT- RULES—Federal Maritime Law rules, used for maritime actions in federal courts, but please note that this does not include Local Rules for Admiralty Cases in the various district courts in the U.S.

FMIL-RULES—Federal Military Law rules for military appellate courts.

FSEC-RULES—Federal Securities Law - Rules, used for administrative actions and requests involving the Securities Exchange Commission.

FTX-RULES—Federal Taxation rules are general rules for tax court matters, found in Title 26 of the U.S. Code, but there may be local tax court rules to look for in the xx-RULES database.

US-RULESCOMM—Federal Rules of Practice & Procedure Advisory Committee Minutes. These are the minutes of the standing committees on the various rules which are charged with drafting and amending the federal rules, and who advise and report to the Judicial Conference Advisory Committee. Coverage begins in 1992 and 1993. You can limit your search to committee minutes on one set of rules using the citation (ci) field; e.g., if you only want minutes of the committee on the Fed. R. Civ. P., you can add "ci(frcp)" to your search.

FPP—Wright and Miller's treatise, Federal Practice & Procedure, can be searched at FPP.

C.   Other federal rules

Certain rules pertain to specific types (subject matter) of actions.

Bankruptcy: Rules for conducting actions in the United States Bankruptcy Court are found in Title 11 of the U.S. Code.

Taxation: Rules of Practice and Procedure for the United States Tax Court are found in Title 26 of U.S. Code (the Internal Revenue Code).

International Trade: Rules of procedure in the United States Court of International Trade are found in the Appendix to Title 28 of the U.S. Code.

The Appendix to Title 28 also includes certain "local rules" for particular courts; e.g., the Rules of the Supreme Court of the United States, Rules of the United States Court of Federal Claims, the General Rules of the Temporary Emergency Court of Appeals of the United States.

PRACTICE POINTER

Local Rules are extremely important, perhaps more important than you can get your head around at such an early stage of your career. We have witnessed briefs getting "bounced" or even important motions outright denied for failure to follow a court's local rules regime. You *must* consult the local rules of the court in which you are filing any document before you file it. In fact, we recommend (short of regaling you with horror stories) that you comb over the local rules of the court (or even the particular judge's chambers) in which you are filing before you file something. In all honesty, even the failure to include what you might consider to be merely a pro-forma document can be the difference between whether a document is accepted or rejected by the court.

D.　Secondary sources for commentary, interpretation of rules

The **Judicial Advisory Committee Notes** that are printed following the text of each rule in the U.S. Code, U.S.C.A., U.S.C.S., each West pamphlet, and most every other volume on the rules, are a secondary persuasive authority, and are considered to be highly persuasive. They are not "drafting history" per se; you would cite to the Advisory Committee Notes as a contemporaneous construction and explanation of what the rules mean, rather than evidence of drafter's intent.

The **Practice Commentaries** for certain rules that are printed in some of West's publications and on Westlaw are the same type of commentary and construction of the rules from a practical viewpoint, but are less persuasive than the Advisory Committee Notes above.

We've talked about **Wright & Miller's <u>Federal Practice and Procedure</u>** (West), before. It is very useful, and now it is on-line in Westlaw's FPP database. Its competitors include: <u>Moore's Federal Practice</u> (Matthew Bender), <u>Federal Litigation Guide</u> (Matthew Bender), <u>West's Federal Practice Manual</u> (West), <u>Federal Procedure, Lawyers Edition</u> (West, formerly Lawyers Coop), <u>Cyclopedia of Federal Procedure</u> (West, formerly Lawyers Coop).

<u>**Weinstein's Evidence**</u> is a good volume on evidence in general and the Federal Rules of Evidence in particular.

II.　FEDERAL AND STATE COURT LOCAL RULES

Court Copies—The best place to get a copy of the local rules is from the court itself. Very often the courts give them away, or they may charge a nominal fee for the paper. These copies should be considered an official version of the rules, but always ask if there are any **administrative orders** issued by the court (see Court Orders above) that have modified the rules or procedures of the court since the publication of the set of rules they are giving out. These administrative orders are usually available in slip copy form at the clerk's office if you ask for them. In recent years, courts have been posting (and updating) their local rules on their websites

– however, you always should double check to make sure you have the most recent version.

West Pamphlets—West yearly puts out very useful pamphlets of local rules of state and federal courts identified by the state's name; <u>e.g.</u>, **New Jersey Court Rules**, **Washington Court Rules**. They are a companion to the federal general rules pamphlets discussed above. The local rules of the federal courts in the state typically are included, as are the state's general rules of procedure for state courts in the state. Periodically, the local rules of each of the state trial courts (<u>e.g.</u>, Local Rules of the 22nd Judicial Circuit, St. Louis City) will be printed, but not every year. The pamphlets are sometimes updated during the year with a paste-in pocket part, if the rules incur very significant changes. Lastly, you can try a West-law database, **xx-RULES**, where the xx represents the state's initials; e.g. NY-RULES. These xx-RULES databases contain the local rules for state courts and federal courts located in a state.

III.   STATE GENERAL RULES OF PROCEDURE

The states' general rules of procedure often can be found in the *official* state statutes, but <u>not</u> always. For example, you will not find the Missouri Supreme Court Rules anywhere in the Missouri Revised Statutes.

You will almost always find the state rules in the *annotated* version of the state statutes; <u>e.g.</u>, you will find the **Missouri Supreme Court Rules** printed in **Vernon's Annotated Missouri Statutes** (West), and in pamphlet editions such as **Missouri Court Rules** discussed above. Naturally, the annotated statutes will provide annotations to the rules. The pamphlet editions (<u>e.g.</u>, Missouri Court Rules) do not have annotations.

IV.   DRAFTING REPORTS ("LEGISLATIVE HISTORY") OF THE FEDERAL RULES

Records of the U.S. Judicial Conference: Committees on Rules of Practice and Procedure (Congressional Information Service)—CIS, the legislative history maven, has collected the records of the committees drafting the rules. Ultimately the rules are approved and promulgated by order of the United States Supreme Court. As noted above, the Advisory Committee Notes are not really drafting history and are not considered to be evidence of the drafter's intent. Instead, they are a contemporaneous construction of the rules, but are held to be very persuasive.

Federal Rules Service; Federal Rules Decisions—these volumes will print various reports and commentary that precede the promulgation of rules or are contemporaneous with the rules. If the report is from a member of the drafting committee, or the committee itself, or from a Supreme Court justice who voted on the rule, it can be used like "legislative history." E.g., a Supreme Court justice might write a piece on a new federal rule and what it means, which is akin to a legislative subcommittee/committee report or conference committee report on legislation, because it is a discussion of the meaning of the rule from a person who actually voted on the rule.

Drafting History of the Federal Rules of Criminal Procedure— volumes devoted to the drafting history of the Federal Rules of Criminal Procedure.

Federal Rules of Evidence: Legislative Histories and Related Documents—volumes devoted to the legislative and drafting history of the Federal rules of Evidence.

V.   CITATOR SERVICES

Shepard's has several volumes which attempt to track the cases citing the rules—**Federal Rules Citations; United States Citations-Statutes, Shepard's Citations** for the various states; **Shepard's Federal Law Citations in Selected Law Reviews**.

The U.S.C.A., U.S.C.S., and other volumes track cases citing the rules, but they do not sort them in terms of positive or negative treatment. If a rule drastically is reinterpreted by a case in your jurisdiction, you will have to search through the entire annotations list to find it.

On-line, Westlaw's rules databases are based on U.S.C.A. and the companion state volumes, like Vernon's Annotated Missouri Statutes, so you will get annotations to the cases citing the rule.

VI.   SUBJECT-SPECIFIC ON-LINE RESOURCES

One way to search the fee-based on-line services is by topic rather than by jurisdiction. More often than not, this is a strategy best employed when you are doing background research to familiarize yourself with an area of law or when you are researching a non-jurisdiction specific legal problem, such as a law review article or a fifty-state survey (by the way, both Westlaw and Lexis have collected fifty-state surveys on various topics). Topical databases are ***not*** a starting and finishing point for research into a specific client's matter in a specific jurisdiction because you may exclude relevant, controlling authority from the applicable jurisdiction if you limit your search to topical databases. Westlaw and Lexis both are set up to accommodate this kind of search.

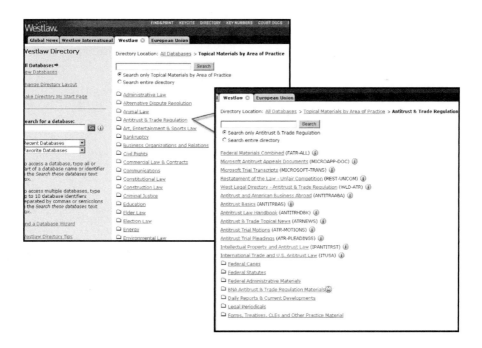

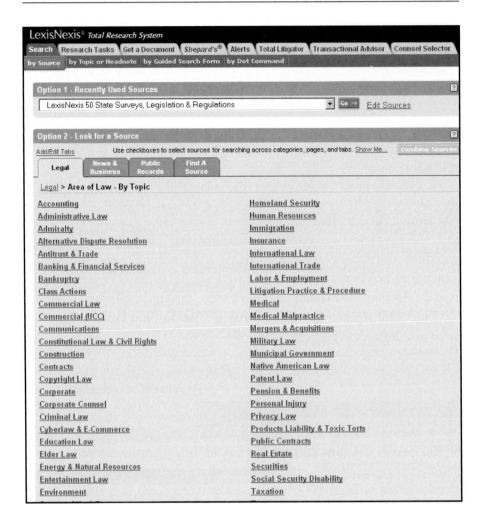

VII.   SUBJECT-SPECIFIC PRINT RESOURCES

A.   Loose-leaf services

Loose-leaf service are generally binders or newsletters whose goal is to keep practitioners up to speed in a specific area of the law. They are especially useful for areas that have a lot of administrative law, and in which the law (rules, regulations, legal standards) change frequently. E.g., employment law, labor law, tax law, securities law.

If the rules, regs, opinion letters, service bulletins, and other material comes out thick and fast in your area of the law, you cannot always rely on your own skills (or your partners', associates', or librarian's skills) in staying abreast of what the law is in a heavily regulated and active area. You subscribe to a loose-leaf service instead, and rely on it (the publisher and its team of editors and researchers) to do the leg work for you so that you can browse an executive summary or pick up an index and go right to the material that answers your legal questions.

The services strive to **collect** resources, **edit and organize** the information, and especially perform **indexing** of the material. This is what you pay for in a loose-leaf service. The full text of cases, laws, rules, and regulations, and significant legislative history information often are reported in the volumes. Tables of cases, statutes, regulations, and cross-references to the same are popular, too. Often reports and editorials will accompany each release, and summarize and alert you to new developments reported therein so that you can tell at a glance if you need to dig into a periodic release of information. They are increasingly found on Westlaw and Lexis. *E.g.*, almost all BNA publications are on Lexis and Westlaw, and a few of the CCH titles are as well.

B.   Types of loose-leaf service

- Newsletters

- Binders with Interfiled Pages

- Combination of the Two

A regular newsletter will produce reports and information about the area of law on a periodic basis (weekly, bi-weekly, monthly, etc.). Contents include new court cases, new administrative rules and regulations, opinion letters, previews of upcoming law, editorial comments, recent state and federal developments, and more. You can browse through the publication each period, or wait until you have an issue and go to an index and see what transpired since the last time you looked at this particular area.

Binders with interfiled pages collect and organize the law in one place for you. When the law changes, the publisher issues new pages to replace the ones that have become outdated—reporting the new laws, new rules and regs that now apply, taking out the old ones that have been superseded or abrogated, giving notice of new cases, bulletins, opinion letters, and other interpretations that have come down.

The updating can be periodic (e.g., weekly, monthly), or done on an "as-needed" basis. The updating is done by a team of researchers and editors at the publisher (e.g., Federal Securities Law Reporter, Copyright Law Reporter, Antitrust & Trade Regulation Report) or is handled by one particular author or editor and his or her researchers (e.g., Newberg on Class Actions, Moore's Federal Practice). These latter volumes are often referred to as "**treatises**," although they operate just like any other loose-leaf publication.

Commerce Clearing House (CCH), Bureau of National Affairs (BNA), Clark Boardman Callaghan, Matthew Bender, Research Institute of America (RIA), Pike & Fischer, West, Aspen, and LEXIS Law are the leading publishers of topical, subject-matter specific publications.

Chapter 8

Bringing it All Together: Strategies for Research and Determining When You are Finished

This chapter is a capstone for the research process. We will review the planning and strategizing required for research, we will give you additional hints on how to use the fee-based research services and free internet sources effectively and efficiently, and we will discuss research plans for when you have less than an infinite amount of time to complete your research and report your results. Lastly, we will give you some practical pointers for how to determine when you are finished with a given research project.

We begin with a summary of the research strategies first introduced in Chapter 1, including the stages of planning for research and the execution of the plan.

I.   INITIAL ASSESSMENT OF THE PROBLEM

Your first job is to assess the problem so as to identify the issues— the specific legal questions that need to be answered—and then to determine if additional facts are needed from the client or other sources, and finally to put together a plan of action to find the legal sources necessary to answer the questions.

A.   What is at issue?

You may have an idea about which areas of the law are implicated by the problem (*e.g.*, this sounds like a fraud case, or this is probably a copyright case), but you often will not necessarily know enough about these areas and their fundamental background principles, claims, defenses, and policies to be able to determine the specific legal questions you will need to answer. You may not even know the general areas of the law implicated by the problem. Assuming the assigning attorney or the client cannot shed any light on this, you will need to do initial background research into the appropriate area of law.

B.   Background research into the area of law

When you have a background resource, you will read it to answer the following questions:

- What are the major issues in this area of the law, both old and new?

- What are the kinds of claims, injuries, damages, causes of action, or defenses that are brought or claimed or asserted in this area?

- What constitutional issues are implicated (if any)?

- Are there statutes, rules, or administrative regulations that typically are found in this area?

The information that you find in a dictionary or encyclopedia may help you get your feet wet, but you may exhaust what they have to say on your matter without determining the actual issues that are implicated by your facts. You will have to go deeper, to hornbooks, treatises, and practice guides.

At the end of your crash course in the area of law, you need to be able to return to your set of facts and determine the specific questions that are presented by these facts. If you cannot do this, return to the background material. You might also discover a need for additional factual information.

C.   Background research into the facts

If you determine that your boss or the client did not give you enough factual information to answer the issues intelligently, go back and ask for more information. Assuming the well is dry, or the professor who assigned the work will not tell you anything else, you will perform your research with what you already know, or turn to alternative sources of factual information.

D.   Background information of the "how to do it" kind

The background information you need may simply consist of "how to" information in an area of law. "How to" sources include your colleagues and other attorneys (in real life, not law school), practice guides and CLE materials, the actual agency or court involved, or pleading and practice form books.

II.   PLANNING YOUR RESEARCH

After formulating the questions you must answer, *you must come up with a plan* for finding the sources to answer each issue. You should divide your plan into categories—how are you going to find:

- Primary controlling authorities

- Primary persuasive authorities

- Secondary authorities

- Sources for checking and validating your authorities.

It is advisable actually to write up a plan of action and follow it. Write down the sources you will use and the order in which you will use them. Leave space in your plan outline to make notes on what you checked. Keep a good record of every item (every individual authority) that you find, including what it says and the citation and page number. This last piece of advice will save you hours of frustration in the future when you cannot find the same book on the shelf, or the library is closed, or you cannot quite remember the name of the case that said something crucial about a certain element of a legal rule.

A well prepared record of the findings also can be used as a skeleton outline of your written work product, which you later can flesh out and turn into a proper treatment of the issues. For example, as you research, you probably will learn that there are X number of required elements for the issue, and 2 or 3 exceptions to the rule, and X number of defenses to the rule. Writing them down in your notes on what you are finding will create a skeleton outline of the Rule section of your written work product. As you find authorities that provide the sub-rules, factors, policies, considerations, or simply provide explanation or clarification of any of the items in the outline, you can fill in the information in the proper sections of the treatment of the main issue and elements as you proceed along in your research. Then, when you stop, you will have a fairly complete skeleton outline of the actual work product you will draft. If you can fill in the skeleton outline on a laptop computer as you go along, even better.

III.   PERFORMING THE RESEARCH

A.   What determines the scope of the research?

You cannot always adopt a "leave no stone unturned" plan in which you will try to completely exhaust every possible source for the law. Sometimes the deadline set by your boss or the court is too short for that; other times, the client simply cannot or will not afford that level of research. Time and money are important factors in actual law practice.

Another factor is your knowledge of the area of the law. If you know the area well, you will not have to look for authorities in as many places, and you can zero in on the sources you know are likely to lead you directly to the answer. When you are familiar with the area, you will feel more confident when you think you have found the right answer and can stop. The converse is true when you are less familiar with the area of law— you will need to look to more sources to find authorities and may not be as confident that you are done with the research.

B.   Sample research plans

There is no perfect research plan, but some plans are better than others. If you have endless amounts of time and no money issues to constrain you, you could spend weeks and often months researching almost any issue of law. The more time you spend, the more likely it is that you will find, review, and analyze every important source on the law in the area. But no one—no law student, no law professor, and certainly no practitioner—has unlimited time for research. Accordingly, the advice below is directed toward helping you put together a *practical* research plan, not a perfect plan. The sample plans here will guide you through the steps of your research and refer you to the sources you should consult along the way. By following an appropriate plan for the time frame (or money constraints) of your situation, you will allow yourself the greatest opportunity to find all of the relevant authorities and not miss something important.

Research is broader than writing. Every plan described below will ask you to look at a greater number of authorities than you will wind up writing about in your office memorandum or court brief. You must read broadly and check and recheck your findings in a variety of ways in order to determine what the law is; then you present it in writing using the most authoritative, most telling, and most illustrative authorities.

Below we provide several examples of research plans. Plan 1 discusses the steps necessary to do proper research involving a statute, rule, or administrative regulation, and Plans 2 to 5 supplement that with case law and secondary source research.

1. Plan 1—When a statute, rule, or administrative regulation is involved

These steps are required for researching statutes, rules, or regulations. You cannot skip these steps even if you are in one of the pinched-for-time scenarios discussed below. Plans 2 to 5 are the additional steps needed to research case law and secondary sources that will be added on to the research after you have worked through the steps of this initial plan.

a. When a statute or rule or regulation applies, you must start with the statute, rule, or regulation in your research. Read carefully what it says.

b. Review an annotated version of the statute or rule—this will show you cases citing the statute or rule, and it will note cases that add, change, explain, modify, or distinguish the statute or rule. Read the cases that are on the topic that you are researching. They should be organized in the annotations by topic or sub-topic.

c.   Research the administrative regulations, the administrative rules that implement the regulations, and any "official" and unofficial interpretations by administrative and executive entities charged with implementing the regulation (the agency itself, the attorney general, a regulatory body or commission).

d.   If there appear to be divergent opinions in the authorities you are reading about the meaning or application of certain provisions of the statute or regulation, then you should note that research into the legislative history of the statute or drafting and ratification history of the rule or regulation may be necessary. You may not have time to do this step right away, but you should plan to complete it as soon as possible.

e.   Then move on to the cases and secondary authorities as provided in the plans below.

2.   **Plan 2—When you have lots of time (and expense is not an issue), whether or not you are familiar with this area of law** [the "more than a week" research plan].

a.   You can be as thorough as you want. If you are unfamiliar with the law, then start with the restatement (if there is one on this topic), and then a top notch treatise. Then move on to an ALR or two.

b.   If a statute, rule, or administrative regulation is on point, work through the steps of Plan 1 above. Read the cases cited in the annotations on your topic. Use Westlaw or Lexis or the digests to find even more cases. Shepardize or KeyCite your cases to find even more cases, and read them; then Shepardize or KeyCite the new cases.

c.   Move on to a different treatise (if there is one), and perhaps a third treatise. Make sure you are arriving at the correct rules of law regarding your issue by cross-checking with more than one treatise authority. Note that even here, you are not attempting to read the treatise or restatement cover to cover. This would be virtually impossible. You are looking at the applicable sections or chapters that cover your topic.

d.   Read several law review articles on point. Note any current developments, emerging issues, and changes in the law. Read the articles critically, and attempt to distinguish the author's "take" on the law—her views, criticisms, recommendations, and predictions—from the actual prevailing legal principles discussed in the article. You should be most interested in the latter.

e.   Read a recent CLE publication on this topic to make sure you have the most up-to-date information about the law—the breaking news stories, the most recent developments. Of course, you also have been checking the pocket parts, supplements, and advance sheets of the reporters, treatises, and ALRs as you go along.

f.   Shepardize or KeyCite your cases again. Check the good cases and the bad cases. Read every citing authority.

g.   Re-read your best authorities one more time. Be sure you understand them and get all of your notes and citations (and page numbers) in order.

h.   If you've got the money to spend—yours or your client's—make copies of every authority (i.e., the whole case, or the relevant pages of the treatise, restatement, law review or ALR) that you think you might use to write up your results; both the authorities that go your way and the authorities that do not.

3.   Plan 3—When you cannot or do not want to spend much time, but you are well familiar with this area of the law [the "2-5 day" research plan]**.**

a.   Go for the jugular—try first to find controlling primary authorities.

i.   If a statute, rule, or administrative regulation is on point, work through the steps of Plan 1 above. Read the cases cited in the annotations on your topic. The use Westlaw, Lexis, or Digests and look for cases on point. You may get the answer right here, right now.

ii.   Quickly consult a treatise or restatement as a check to make sure your results are in line with established authority.

iii.   Check a CLE publication, ALR, or even one or more law review articles just to make sure there has not been a significant new change in the law in the last few months.

iv.   Research other secondary sources?—Probably not enough time, but do so if you know of one specifically on point (especially one specific to a specialized area of law).

b.   Verify and validate your authorities with Shepard's or KeyCite.

4.   Plan 4—You cannot or do not want to spend much time, but you are NOT familiar with this area of the law

This is a conundrum. You need the time but you do not have the time.

a. If the issue is money, not time per se, consider doing the background research described above as non-billed time.

b. If the issue really is time—"I only have X days to do this"— reverse the plan so that you at least read the restatement or a treatise first, and then do the Plan 1 research for a problem involving a statute, rule, or administrative regulation, and then run case law searches on-line or with digests. In this way, you have a better chance of figuring out the big picture—all the issues and defenses and constitutional problems—before zeroing in on individual cases.

c. Do not fail to verify your sources with Shepard's or KeyCite—you will not do anyone any good if you report bad law to them.

5. Plan 5—No real time at all, whether or not you are familiar with this area of law [the "few hours to a day" plan]

a. You will be rushed to complete the steps of the statutory, rule, or administrative law research required for Plan 1 above, but there is no way around those steps in problems involving this kind of primary authority. In this modern legal world, statutes, rules, and administrative law often are involved in even a simple research problem.

b. After Plan 1's steps are completed, *you must zero in quickly on finding the most relevant cases that you haven't yet collected using the annotations to the statute or rule.* Use the on-line services or digests, find the most current and most relevant cases, and Shepardize or KeyCite them to find more cases (as well as to make sure they still are good law).

c. Squeeze in one good treatise or the restatement just to make sure you have not missed the big picture or omitted a crucial point about the law in your analysis.

Of course, the fifth plan is highly risky, and we are not recommending that you use it in law school as you learn the process of legal research. You can miss important things by moving so fast, especially if you were not that familiar with the area of law to begin with. That said, you will not always have the luxury of checking and rechecking a broad range of authorities, and so we wanted to present you with the most bare boned option for reaching an answer (which you likely will have to qualify by saying that it is just an initial stab at the material, or a quick-and-dirty impression). Do what you can in an intelligent manner. And always, always Shepardize or KeyCite your good and bad authorities.

PRACTICE POINTER

Lest you think we are being unrealistic (or irresponsible) for even including this quick-and-dirty research plan, we wanted to offer a quick anecdote from practice. You may find, as we both did, that some clients will ask for an initial read on a situation so that they can decide whether to proceed with a full-blown investigation or even so that they can go into a meeting armed with an educated guess as to how they might fare should they actually bring a piece of litigation. These are the types of situations in which you may only have an hour (or only be authorized to spend an hour) attempting to get your head around a legal issue.

IV.   ADVANCED SEARCH TECHNIQUES ON WESTLAW AND LEXIS

In previous chapters, we introduced the basics of research using Westlaw and Lexis in a variety of research situations, and presumably you also will receive training from your law school's Westlaw or Lexis representatives on basic research strategies. These techniques, once mastered, will carry you through a great deal of the research you will have to perform in your life and law practice, but Westlaw and Lexis also have important additional search features that can help you narrow down results and zero in on the most helpful authorities sooner.

A.   Field and segment searching

Field searching is an *excellent* way of limiting the number of cases you might otherwise pull up in a search. You can restrict your search to one part of a document, known in Westlaw as a "field" and in Lexis as a "segment" (*e.g.,* just the synopsis that starts off the case, just the title or style of the case, or just the headnotes).

In Westlaw, if you want to search certain parts of the document, you can code your searches as follows:

co	Searches the court field—what the name of the court is. You put what you are looking for in parentheses.
	co(nj) searches for courts having a connection to New Jersey
sy	Searches only the synopsis field — the West summary at the beginning of the case.
	sy(neglig!) searches the synopsis for forms of the term "negligence" "negligent" etc.
he	Searches the headnotes for a term.
	he(copyright) searches the headnotes for the term "copyright"
to	Searches the Topic field from the West list of topics from the digest series.
ti	Title or style of the case, the parties.
	ti(roe & wade) searches for titles of cases with Roe and Wade in them
	ti(roe +s wade) searches for titles where Roe precedes Wade
di	Searches the headnotes for a term.

You can use them in combination by separating with a comma:

to,he,sy(neglig!)   searches   the   Topic,
Headnotes,   and   Synopsis   fields   for
variations on the term "negligence"

sy,di   is a particularly useful combined
field-restrictive search that will help you
limit the universe of cases that you generate
to only those that are the most relevant.

There are quite a few more fields—consult your Westlaw materials or ask your Westlaw representative.

Lexis has a similar concept called "Segments" which are searched by choosing segments on the search screen and filling in the terms you want the authorities to possess within those segments (see Lexis illustration in the next section).

B.   Date restrictions

Often you only will want to pull up cases before or after a certain date, or within a certain range of dates. Westlaw and Lexis have made this simple by working options to set up date restrictions right into their search screens:

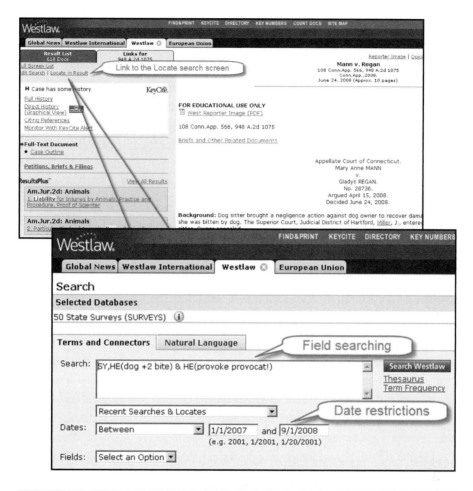

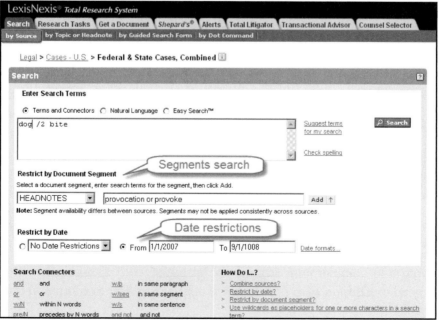

If you decide to do a restriction in the actual search query on Westlaw, you would do it in this way:

da   A date restriction. You can limit to a single
                            date or before or after a given date. In
                            combination, you can set a range of dates.
                            (You must use a four-digit year due to Y2K
                            compliance.)

With all three forms here, you only will get cases after Jan. 1, 1998

da(after 01/01/1998)

da(aft 01/01/1998)

da(> 01/01/1998)

These three will get cases before Jan. 1, 1988

da(before 01/01/1988)

da(bef 01/01/1988)

da(< 01/01/1988)

This form will get cases from 1997

da(1997)

This combination will get cases from the 1980's

da(>01/01/80) & da(<01/01/90)

Date restrictions and field searches are added to a search query with an &:

dog +2 bite & co,sy(il) & da(aft 01/01/1965)

C.   Searching for particular headnotes (keynotes)

On Westlaw, the topic name of a keynote (<u>e.g.</u>, Contracts) is replaced by its number on the master list of key note topics (95), and the key symbol (⚷) is replaced by the letter "k"

95k23	Will get you cases with that headnote (keynote) number in it, Contracts: Qualified or conditional acceptance of offer
95k88	Will get you cases with the headnote, Contracts: Presumptions and burden of proof

You can search for all notes under one topic:

to(95), to(contracts)   Both forms will get you contracts cases.

If you want to search a particular topic for terms within a headnote:

to(95) /p (breach /2 implied /3 covenant /4 good faith fair dealing)

This search string will get you all cases with a contracts headnote that contains the terms "breach of covenant of good or faith or fair or dealing"

D.   Locate (or focus)

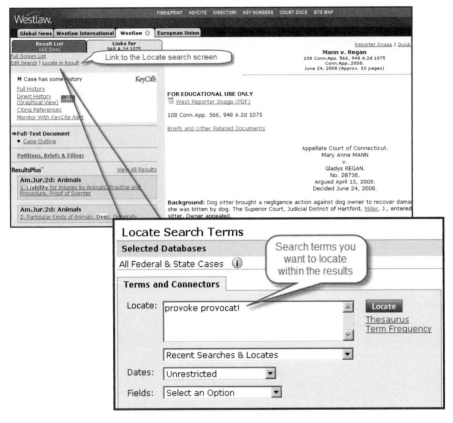

Once you have your search results, and you really want to zero in on the most important cases, you can run a search within a search on Westlaw (called "Locate") or on Lexis (called "Focus"). You would formulate a Locate query in the same way as a regular search query, with terms and connectors, fields, dates, headnotes, and any other search addition:

95k125 & date(>07/15/1988) This Locate query would zero in on documents within your search results that contain Contracts headnotes with key number 125, and are dated after July 15, 1988.

V.   ADVICE ON NATURAL LANGUAGE SEARCHING

In an effort to simplify (perhaps over-simplify) the requirements for searching the on-line services, both Westlaw and Lexis came up with a simplified method referred to as "Natural Language" searching. West-law calls it "Natural Language" searching and Lexis has two versions, one called "Natural Language" and the other "Easy Search" searching. In all three cases, you simply enter a sentence or short phrase that sums up your research topic without regard to logic or synonyms or connections, and Westlaw or Lexis finds you cases that have as many of those words in it as it can. (Easy Search on Lexis is supposed to work best with short searches of just a few words). The service assumes each word is connected by an "and" (&) connector. The service ignores certain words (an, but, the, etc.). Results are limited to twenty (or however many you tell it to get), and results are sorted by statistical relevance (unless you tell it to sort by some other way); *e.g.*, the more times your terms appear in a document and the closer proximity they appear to each other in the document bumps the document up on the list of results. Basically, it works like many Internet search engines—Google and Excite, for example.

If you run the following search,

Is a hunter liable when he accidentally shoots someone in her home

the service probably will ignore "is, a, when, he, in, her" and sort the cases that have hits on the remaining words.

Though this type of searching may sound appealing, there are several reasons why you generally should avoid Natural Language searching:

A.   It is not logical enough.

You are doing legal research, not surfing the net for recreation or wikis. You are not just trying to find twenty odd cases having several of your search terms in them; you are trying to find ***all*** of the relevant, time-ly, controlling authorities. You can make a much more accurate search with Boolean logic connectors and the methods described in the chapters above.

B.   It does not find synonyms.

This is crucial. If an important controlling authority from your jurisdiction (or worse yet, a line of controlling authorities) expressed the law in slightly different terms than you put in your natural search, you will fail to uncover some directly relevant (and, most likely, some highly analogous) authorities.

C.   You cannot be certain you have exhausted the field.

With just "and" (&) as the connection, you will not want to run searches such as "dog bite." You can run twenty different natural language searches, but that is wasting your time. You can do a better search with terms and connectors the first time. Just spend a few more minutes coming up with a good list of search words and synonyms and create a search with logic connectors.

VI.   ADVICE ON USING FEE-BASED ON-LINE SERVICES VERSUS FREE INTERNET SITES

In order to appreciate the transition from on-line legal research using fee-based services to research using the free resources and services of the Internet, you must consider the benefits of the former services and compare them to the detriments of the latter. Westlaw and Lexis offer the following:

• High price - high expectations.

No one will argue with you if you assert that Westlaw and Lexis are expensive. But you get a reliable, high quality product for your money. The price you pay begs high expectations for foolproof research assistance, and Westlaw and Lexis both fulfill these expectations.

• Reputations that are tested by tens of thousands of users.

Nearly every attorney in the United States has used Westlaw and Lexis. Thousands, if not tens of thousands of attorneys use the services every day. If there ever were to be a glitch in the services (beyond the usual frustration of getting slow service at times) or in their coverage of legal information, it would be revealed by thousands of users and corrected as soon as possible.

• Westlaw and Lexis are in stiff competition with each other.

At this point in time, there is not much of a difference between Westlaw and Lexis, and both services have an enormous incentive to keep it that way. Each would like to gain an edge, but it is more important for each to maintain parity in the legal information arms race. The customer benefits from this life and death competition, because services are kept fresh, new databases are added all the time, existing coverage is extended, and material is updated and kept current, all so that customers are kept satisfied.

• Westlaw and Lexis constantly are updated and kept current.

As mentioned in the previous section, neither fee-based service can afford to let the other gain an edge in current materials, so each service keeps their databases as up to date as possible. What this means is that statutes are available the moment that they are passed into law, cases are added to the databases within hours or at least within a day or two of their issuance, and databases constantly are expanded and kept current.

Now compare the above factors to the free resources and services of the Internet and World Wide Web:

• The Internet is free.

It's true, you cannot beat the price.

• Reputation?

Some Internet sites have some history and track record to them. Some are admired for the accuracy and usefulness of their information. But when you replace a profit-making incentive and a life or death struggle to survive (Westlaw and Lexis) with an altruistic desire to do well and benefit all mankind (most Internet sites), you do not necessarily get the very best service. Sometimes you get what you pay for.

There is very little peer review from practicing lawyers concerning Internet legal research sites unless you want to go far out of your way to find out what some Internet gazetteers or reference librarians are saying about a site. The average attorney will not want to spend time tracking down the dirt on each site before she uses it and relies on it. Even if a few sites are investigated thoroughly, there is no guaranty that they will stay accurate and up to date.

• Competition? Quality control?

There is no real competition between the services that provide free legal information on the Internet. It is true that some sites, such as Findlaw.com., do accept advertising. These sites might hope to raise advertising revenue based on the number of hits, so market forces have some role, but the scale of attraction of new users vs. potential loss of users if your site has or develops some shortcomings is so small in comparison to the battle between Westlaw and Lexis that it does not propel too many web management decisions. Most sites just exist to provide information with no real hope of making any money in the process. Many sites want to excel in the accuracy and coverage of their information as a matter of academic or institutional pride, but there is little to be done to regulate the quality of sites that do not share this zeal for excellence. A few sporadic visitors checking out the free merchandise are not going to police a site's content, accuracy, and up-to-datedness.

• You can put ANYTHING on the Internet

Probably the most alarming fact about the Internet is that anyone can post "legal" information on the Internet and World Wide Web and make it available to anyone searching for legal information. Whether or not the publisher makes an effort to publicize it, sooner or later search engines will find it and catalog it, and it will show up in searches. No one regulates the posting of information on the web. No one controls it. No official body reviews it for quality, content, and accuracy. No one guarantees that the legal or factual information on sites is good enough to use to render legal advice to clients under a **legal malpractice** standard.

Speaking of malpractice, consider the fact that lawyers, judges, and bar disciplinary people all know that lawyers use Westlaw or Lexis, and that it is a perfectly acceptable and reliable way to do legal research. Using these systems in a reasonable manner will not get you into trouble. In fact, refusing to use them may be more problematic in some situations than using them too much, because a disgruntled client may assert that you failed to do proper research when you avoided these modern, up-to-the minute research tools.

- You cannot count on proper updating and maintenance of sites.

Updating of sites and keeping them current is a real problem for many websites. It takes an enormous amount of time and effort to update all of your pages. The bigger and better a legal site gets, the more it needs to be updated to keep it great. Westlaw and Lexis make that investment of time and effort. Does Cornell Law Library or the federal Government Printing Office have the resources or time to do it as well?

VII. APPROPRIATE USES OF THE INTERNET AS A TOOL FOR LEGAL RESEARCH

A. Background information.

You always can use the Internet as a starting point to get your feet wet in a research project and not rack up extra fees for the client. You can find certain primary and secondary legal sources, factual information, and background information to move you to an understanding of the issues and policies before you dive in to do the direct research to address the problem at hand.

B. The Internet can be used as the primary tool for legal research in the following instances:

- When you are looking for a particular item.

If what you need to find is one particular thing, such as a case, a statutory provision, or a federal administrative regulation, and you know what it is called, and you know what it will look like, so that when you pull it up you will know you found it, then the Internet is every bit as effective as Westlaw or Lexis. Findlaw.com. for example, is a perfectly effective way to get an electronic copy of a case whose cite you know.

- When you already have a very good idea what the answer to your research problem is, and you are researching merely to confirm what you already know.

Knowing the answer ahead of time is a rare luxury for a lawyer. When it happens that you have become familiar with the correct answer to a certain kind of legal problem, but you would like to browse a few sources to make sure your memory is not playing tricks on you, using the Internet for this limited purpose is fairly safe.

- When it does not really matter what you find, as long as you find something.

There are situations in legal practice where gathering a small but representative sample of authorities will suffice to address the problem at hand. In the middle of trial, you do not need to find all fifty cases in your jurisdiction that say that proof of collateral sources of compensation such as insurance coverage generally is inadmissible in a personal injury case if all you need is one or two cases to remind the judge of the law and to convince her that you are not making this up. When you are drafting a brief, and you want to state an undisputable black letter law proposition, and you simply want to find one case from your jurisdiction that has said this proposition, using the Internet to track down a case is generally fine.

C.   The Internet <u>should not</u> be used as the primary tool for legal research in the following instances:

- When you are researching a problem for a client that requires you to find and interpret all of the relevant and applicable law in your jurisdiction in order to render correct, reliable, legal advice.

If a client is counting on you to find and analyze all of the relevant authorities in order to render correct legal advice, you should not step to the plate and try to hit a hardball with a whiffle ball bat. You might get the bat in just the right position, and one time out of a thousand you will connect and knock the ball out of the park, but the odds are against you. Unfortunately, most of the time, this will be the kind of research problem you will be faced with.

- When you need to verify and confirm that the authorities you are using still are good law.

If one of the main shortcomings of the Internet is that it is not kept up-to-date and not verified for accuracy, then you should never rely on Internet sites to ensure that the authorities you are using still are good law. Go to the Shepard's books or use your persuasive skills to convice the billing partner or the client to let you use Keycite or Shepard's On-line.

- When you really need the answer to the problem quickly.

Westlaw and Lexis will give you a reliable response instantly if you know what questions to ask and where to ask them. No one Internet site can provide you with the complete picture on the average legal issue, so in order to use the Internet more reliably, you must try different sites and cross-check the information you are finding to give yourself a better chance of seeing 90% of the relevant authorities. If we all had enough time to browse twenty sites to make sure we were reading every kind of authority that is accessible on the Internet, then we would significantly reduce the odds of making a huge mistake. But this requires a great deal of time, and time truly is money to a practicing attorney. In fact, almost every time you use the Internet instead of Westlaw or Lexis, you are trading increased research time for cheaper research tools. You might have come out ahead if you simply paid the fee for Westlaw or Lexis and got a reliable answer in much less time.

VIII. HOW DO YOU KNOW WHEN YOU ARE FINISHED?

A tough question, but one that gets easier with experience. Follow this rule of thumb for determining when you are finished with your research:

1. If you have found several (3-5) controlling authorities that agree with each other as to the legal issue at hand, and they are recent enough in time not to give you pause (a good rule of thumb is within the last thirty years for a highest court/highest controlling authority and ten years for an intermediate level appellate court/second highest controlling authority);

2. If you also found several good persuasive authorities that support your controlling authorities, including a treatise or other secondary authority that supports your findings;

3. If you have reconciled or distinguished all contrary controlling authorities and any important persuasive authorities; and

4. If you do not have any nagging questions that you know should be answered before you move on to writing;

Then you are finished!

This is only a rule of thumb. It is not going to hold true in every research problem you encounter in law school or in actual practice. But having some guideline is better than having none. One good piece of advice for applying the rule of thumb is to be on the look out for repetition. Look to see if the sources you are finding are agreeing with each other and citing each other; consider whether you are finding new authorities in your searches or turning up the same set of authorities time after time. If your on-line searches fail to turn up new authorities and your searches in secondary authorities are referring you to sources that you already have read, then you are in a good place to determine that your research is finished. You still will have to read and analyze the authorities you found, but you will not need to keep searching for more authorities to add to your collection. By the same token, if each new search turns up new and unfamiliar authorities, your research is probably not complete.

Each item in the rule of thumb can be further explored, as follows:

A.   Several recent controlling authorities that agree

1.   Finding paydirt!

It is a lovely thing to start your research and find a host of recent controlling authorities that agree on the topic at hand. If they include a statute and several recent cases from the highest authority in the jurisdiction, you will find yourself on Cloud 9. Unfortunately, it will not always be this way.

2.   Not finding anything?

You will not always find a highest court/highest level authority case on point, or you will not find one from the last thirty years. That is okay; it happens from time to time. You may not even find an intermediate level appellate opinion on point. That is rare, but it happens once in a while. Keep looking for controlling authorities. Try new sources, try new ideas, new research terms and topics, but realize that occasionally there simply is no really good controlling authority on point.

3.   How do you "keep looking"?

The key to good research is to *think broadly* and to *think synonyms*. (Another reason why Natural Language searches are almost never the way to go). Broad thinking will allow you to examine the issue in a number of lights, to recast it several times, and eventually to expand on the topics and subjects that you will search under.

Synonyms are the key to proper coverage in research. We cannot rely on clairvoyance to figure out exactly how West Group or other compilers, editors, and authors have categorized the sources you need to find to answer the question. So, you must think of several ways to say the same thing—several subjects, topics and subtopics—in other words, synonyms, so that they will collect all the authorities on point. Sometimes this is an easy call, and sometimes the first topic/subject/subtopic you search under produces paydirt, but not always.

If you need more incentive, this process remains critical when you turn to the computer to do your research. You will need to come up with many synonyms for search terms in order to hit on all the correct authorities. Familiarize with this approach now – it is not just "for the books" (and it doesn't get easier later).

4.   Old cases are not necessarily bad cases.

Do not make up your mind ahead of time that you simply will not write about—will not even cite—any case that is "too old." First of all, it is hard to say what "counts" as old, and it may vary significantly by the area of law you are researching. Relatedly, sometimes "old" is the only game in town.

When we talk about using and writing about "old" authorities, we assume that you have researched well enough to satisfy yourself that there are no other, more recent controlling authorities of the same or higher level court that cover the same area. If there are, then the current, prevailing authorities control (and even if they are not binding, more recent cases tend to be more persuasive). But if "old" cases are the only cases around, then obviously proceed with the old.

The ultimate question always must be: "Is it still good law?" The answer of course depends on how, if at all, the law has changed since the case was decided. You should ask yourself the following questions:

- Is anyone still citing the case for this proposition or for any proposition? Or is it an abandoned derelict on the waters of the law?

- Has the case been abandoned and rejected directly or indirectly by more recent authorities? (i.e., no one is citing it, and other cases with different legal rules and standards are covering this area of the law now.)

- Are the newer cases (perhaps only from the intermediate level court) simply talking a different language (different policies, factors, elements, standards) from that in the earlier case? Has the law moved beyond the old case?

- Has the area of law changed by way of statute or rule since the case was handed down?

5.   Why controlling authorities are of paramount importance.

Controlling authorities are of paramount importance for the obvious reason that they will control the outcome of the issue at hand. You cannot ignore a controlling authority. If it truly is duplicative of other equally or more recent controlling authorities, you very well may not write about it, but you still *must* take it into account in formulating your answer to the research topic. If it is contrary to your other authorities, you must try to reconcile it or distinguish it, and if it cannot be reconciled or distinguished, you must think about changing your "answer" to the legal question you are researching so that the case can work its way into the mix. If it simply cannot work with the other authorities, you have one of those *rare* situations where you may have to craft a rule in such a way as to account for the discrepancy – or hedge a little on what the state of the law is.

6.   Statutes and rules are controlling.

Though statutes and regulations from the applicable jurisdiction are always controlling sources of the law, rarely will they be the last word on a topic.

Statutes and rules typically are written with a view toward the law on the topic that already exists. To the extent that they do not change or supplant the existing law (the rules, sub-rules, legal standards, factors, policies and so forth), but only add to it, then the earlier law (as reflected common law and statutory/rule-based law) continues to have considerable effect and importance.

7.   A whole new regime?

Occasionally, a statute or a whole new set of laws is passed to wipe the entire slate clean and to initiate a new legal regime on a given topic. The Employee Retirement Income Security Act (ERISA) and the Racketeer Influenced and Corrupt Organizations Act (RICO) are examples of this situation. But this genesis effect lasts only until the first court gets a case under the new legal regime; then the court interprets the law, and its opinion becomes part of the law; and the next court interprets the law, and the law has been advanced—at least clarified, perhaps modified, perhaps expanded or diminished. Thus, you must always look for the cases on the topic you are researching, even if it largely is a "statutory" issue.

8.   What are "statutory" research issues?

How do you know when to look for a statute on point? There is no hard and fast rule, but the following are several ways of getting to the right answer.

If the area of the law is one that *traditionally* is regulated by statute (and by the time you graduate, you should have a basic understanding of this kind of area), then you should start looking in the index to the statutes in your jurisdiction for sections that cover your topic. For example, the following areas of state law are traditionally regulated by statute:

Employment (by statutes, rules, and regulations)

Domestic relations

Trusts, estates, wills, intestate succession

Evidence (by rule, rather than statute)

Procedures for legal process and litigation (by statutes or rules)

Criminal law

Public health and safety (building codes, zoning, traffic)

Taxation (by statutes and regulations)

Government—at the state, county, municipal, and local level

Products liability and product safety

Statutes of limitations

Securities, negotiable instruments, checks, promissory notes, etc. (by statutes, rules, and regulations)

Banks, banking, loans and lending, debtor and creditor

Landlord - tenant

Sales of goods (by the UCC, for instance)

There are more than these, but this is a good basic list to start with. If you are not sure, it never hurts to just start with the index to the statutes. If you do not find anything, you can move on.

Almost all federal questions are based on a statute or federal administrative rule or regulation. (As you will learn if you haven't already, there is very little "federal common law"). So, if you have a case governed by federal law (and is not a diversity action—which is most likely going to be governed by state law), then you would be wise to look for the appropriate federal statute(s) on point.

Secondary sources, especially ones that are focused on your jurisdiction, often will highlight and discuss statutes and rules that apply to the topic. This is another good place to start if you are not sure if a statute is involved. Do not ignore state practice guides just because you may never cite them in your final memorandum!

A very good practical tip is to *look at the cases and other authorities you are reading*—if they mention or discuss a statute, then look it up, and see what's going on with it. It may turn out to be entirely tangential or incidental to the problem, but you will never know unless you look it up.

B.   Several good, recent, persuasive authorities

There are several possible reasons why you would want to find and pay attention to recent, persuasive authorities:

1.   Reality check!

If you have found several controlling authorities already, you may only want to examine a few persuasive authorities to make sure your research has not slipped off the deep end—that you have not stumbled into a little dead-end of the law and missed the boulevard that you were supposed to be following. A treatise or other broadly written, comprehensive work can do that. Cases from other jurisdictions can reveal that your jurisdiction's law is followed elsewhere (or not).

2.   Comfort level

Finding a decent treatise that agrees with your findings can be a source of comfort. An ALR or even a law review article can do the trick, too, but it is harder to find one on point. Other materials (CLE publications, practice guides) can be used to make sure your findings are up to date and not out of line with recent trends.

3.   Good authority for big picture, policy issues

As discussed above, secondary sources have many uses other than as authority for briefs. You may want these broader, "big picture" references to make sure you have the lay of the land.

4.   More analogous facts

Looking to cases as persuasive authority is a good way to find a case that is closer to the facts of your own case than any of the controlling cases from your own jurisdiction. These cases will confirm that the law is applied to your client's specific factual situation to produce the results you are reporting, whether or not the actual case is binding authority.

C.   Reconciling/distinguishing authority

You have to reconcile or distinguish controlling authority, as mentioned above. It is a good idea to try to reconcile or distinguish persuasive authority, too, but especially if the authority is "impressive"—a major treatise in the area; a recent case from the highest court of a major state that has reason to handle this area of the law a lot; something written by a highly respected author in this area; anything else receiving high marks as persuasive authority, but which goes against your findings.

D.   Nagging questions?

Your own mind will sometimes tell you that you are not quite finished. If you are wondering whether you need to follow up on a particular factor discussed in several of the cases—because it still isn't making sense to you within the framework of your analysis—you are probably onto something. Should I go research this standard discussed in the cases to see exactly what it means? Should I go and see what this case (or related rule or statute) says? There is no absolute yes or no answer here; you will have to decide if it is worth it. But your conscience may be indicating to you that you should head back to the library.

INDEX

†